MW00651891

There Is More than One Way to Spell Wiener

There Is More than One Way to Spell

WIENER

THE STORY OF NU-WAY

ED GRISAMORE

Foreword by Durwood "Mr. Doubletalk" Fincher

A taste of home for you!

Ed Grisamore

Mercer University Press | Macon, Georgia

MUP/P441

© 2011 Mercer University Press
1400 Coleman Avenue
Macon, Georgia 31207
All rights reserved

First Edition

Books published by Mercer University Press are printed on acid-free paper
that meets the requirements of American National Standard for Information Sciences—
Permanence of Paper for Printed Library Materials.

Mercer University Press is a member of Green Press Initiative (greenpressinitiative.org),
a nonprofit organization working to help publishers and printers increase their use
of recycled paper and decrease their use of fiber derived from endangered forests.
This book is printed on recycled paper.

Book design by Burt&Burt

ISBN 978-0-88146-269-2

Cataloging-in-Publication Data is available from the Library of Congress

Contents

Foreword

Great things don't change.

That's why I have always loved Nu-Way. That's why I always will love Nu-Way.

For as long as I can remember, it has been a part of my personal history with my hometown. I grew up in Macon during the 1950s and '60s. Those were some of the best years of my life. I hold the precious memories dear.

We always went to the Nu-Way on Cotton Avenue, where it all began. For the longest time, that was the only one I knew about. Cotton Avenue was easy to remember, since I was raised in the cotton mill village of Payne City. My mother worked in the mill.

As a youngster, I loved the stools at the Nu-Way, the way they would twist and spin. It was like a little ride. (As you can tell, we didn't have much to do for entertainment in the village.)

Everybody who worked at Nu-Way was friendly. They worked so fast. It was always so clean, cool, and refreshing inside.

But the best thing, of course, was the food. I always got a hot dog and a hamburger.

And I remember that flaky ice. It was their trademark.

My mama, Ella Mae Fincher, was an ice freak. She always thought—and she passed this on to me—it was some of the best ice in the world. She would try to replicate it at home. She would take ice cubes, place them in a towel, and bang it with a hammer.

But she couldn't do it. So she would just go to Nu-Way and eat flaky ice and say things like, "It's a miracle!"

Great things don't change.

Nu-Way was very popular in the village. If anyone was headed in that direction, we would ask them to bring some back. When my brother, Roy, had the car, it was always easy to get up an order and come home with sacks full of hot dogs and hamburgers.

Atlanta has been my home since 1974. I live in Midtown, about fourteen city blocks from The Varsity, a distance of less than two miles. I have to listen to people brag about The Varsity, and I want to tell them Nu-Way would win a taste test every time. They're not even in the same league.

I have introduced a lot of people to Macon by introducing them to Nu-Way. They become instant fans. I got some friends hooked a few years ago, and now every time they go through Macon they have to go to Nu-Way. They once drove back to Atlanta from the beach on a Saturday because they wanted to stop in Macon, and they knew Nu-Way was closed on Sunday.

For several years, I have had "Sittin' on the Dock of the Bay" as the ringtone for my cell phone. People will hear it and recognize it as Otis Redding, who was from Macon. Some will smile and also say, "Nu-Way!"

Great things don't change.

In 2009, I received one of the greatest honors of my life. I was selected grand marshal of the parade for the Cherry Blossom Festival. I was given the key to the city by Mayor Robert Reichert. Of course, my first question to him was, "Does it open the door to the Nu-Way?"

If anyone was going to write a book about Nu-Way, it had to be Ed Grisamore. Nu-Way is a Macon treasure, and Ed is, too. I consider him a true ambassador for this city.

Ed and I began a journey together when he wrote my biography, *Once You Step in Elephant Manure You're in the Circus Forever*. The book was born at the Nu-Way in February 2007. We broke bread, shook hands, and rejoiced over the crunch of flaky ice in the third booth from the door.

And you will rejoice when you read *There Is More than One Way to Spell Wiener*.

Devour every word. It's almost as good as a slaw dog.

Notice I said *almost*. Great things don't change.

—Durwood "Mr. Doubletalk" Fincher

June 2011

Spellbound

There is more than one way to spell wiener.

It has been proven for almost a century.

We can blame it—or bless it—on an unknown Macon sign-painter. In a storefront window along Cotton Avenue, he forgot everything his second-grade teacher taught him about spelling.

"I" before "e" except after "c."

It was the 1930s, and America was in the throes of the Great Depression.

Times were tough. Brother, can you spare a nickel? Maybe the poor guy couldn't afford a dictionary.

In the days before spell-check, the letters would go up in their typographical glory for all the world to see.

"BEST WEINER IN TOWN...NU-WAY WEINER STAND."

In 1937, those letters ascended even higher, more than a story above the sidewalk, hanging from the brick façade of the flagship Macon restaurant. The colorful glass bulbs were like permanent ink, much to the chagrin of English professors and grammarians.

The familiar neon sign has become a downtown landmark, a conversation piece and the ultimate unforgiving text message for those who stop by to satisfy their cravings for chili dogs. It is a point of interest—and even pride—for local historians and community ambassadors.

"You can argue that is the way weiner IS spelled in Macon," said John T. Edge, who grew up with Nu-Ways on his plate and is now the director of the Southern Foodways Alliance at the Center for the Study of Southern Culture at Ole Miss.

Generations of Nu-Way loyalists have dined beneath those misplaced vowels. They have enjoyed chocolate malts with "Weiner" spelled in bold letters across the Styrofoam cups. They have dabbed the mustard from the corners of their mouths with napkins stuffed in sacks printed with no spelling remorse.

"When somebody sees it on the menu for the first time, we have to explain that's the way we spell it!" said third-generation owner Spyros Dermatas.

Other spelling clarifications date back to the beginning of Nu-Way, the second-oldest hot dog stand in America behind Nathan's of Coney Island fame.

Founder James Mallis, who opened the first Nu-Way on Cotton Avenue in February 1916, was a Greek immigrant who bounced across the waves of the Atlantic Ocean aboard a tramp steamer. Like many other Europeans who sailed into New York Harbor and got off the boat at Ellis Island, he spoke little or no English.

His real name was believed to be Demetrios Alexandros Malliotis, although that was somehow lost in translation. His immigration papers were processed as James Mallis, and he began his new life in America missing two vowels and a consonant near the end of his name.

After two years of working as a dishwasher in New York City restaurants and diners, he headed South to the land of grits and honey. He had cousins and friends in Macon, a city originally called "New Town" until it was incorporated in 1823.

In his back pocket, he carried his own special recipe for chili sauce, and he opened a hot dog place in a fruit stand on Cotton Avenue.

It was not the first hot dog establishment in the city, but there was something special about it from the beginning. Mallis promised a "New Way" from "New York" for this "New Town." Only, he altered the spelling to "Nu-Way."

There are those who believe the famous misspelling may have been stenciled on the storefront window about 20 years later. Perhaps a previous sign painter was uneducated, cross-eyed, or had a hangover from the night before.

But, even if he was, there would have been ample opportunity to bring along an eraser when owners George Andros and Gus Lolos finally got together and agreed to put up the neon sign in 1937.

W-E-I-N-E-R had brought Nu-Way plenty of good karma for the more than two decades since Mallis opened the hot dog stand. The two owners, a bit superstitious, weren't about to rock the gravy train.

The major obstacle to buying a new sign was the $500 price tag. They would have to sell almost 10,000 hot dogs at 5 cents each just to break even.

"Weiner" has been misspelled on the famous neon sign at 430 Cotton Avenue since 1937 (Photo by Walter Elliott)

The two owners bickered over the wisdom of the sign. Lolos, an astute and sometimes stubborn businessman, considered the marquee a poor investment. At age twenty-one, Andros had bought half-ownership of the restaurant for $2,400 in 1936. He was a young man of great vision; he was convinced the glowing sign was a revolutionary idea whose time had come and that it would draw in hungry customers like moths to a light.

Blending the art of persuasion with some old-fashioned psychology, Andros was able to convince Lolos he had used him as the inspiration behind the caricature of the chef at the top of the sign.

However, there was no compromise on the spelling of the word "weiner."

"They just laughed and agreed to leave it," said Dermatas. "Years later, there was some discussion about correcting it. But Uncle George was very superstitious. He said it had always been spelled that way and would continue that way. Who were they to play God?"

Or Dog.

Dermatas said the restaurant's management staff still gets letters and e-mails from vendors and customers writing to notify them about a mistake on the company's letterhead and website. The questions can get as stale as a three-day-old bun. When a writer from *Southern Living* came to Macon to write a story about the restaurant, she became somewhat exasperated over the intentional misspelling.

"She couldn't understand why we would spell it that way on purpose," Dermatas said.

The seventy-year-old sign, the oldest functioning neon sign in the city, received a facelift in 2007. (Uncle Gus had gotten a little battered and bruised.) It was refurbished and upgraded with colored glass. The original neon façade is now on display inside the store at the Nu-Way on Zebulon Road.

And, yes, W-E-I-N-E-R is still misspelled.

Mark Twain never ate a Nu-Way hot dog. He lived 800 miles away and died six years before Mallis introduced this culinary creation to the world.

But it somehow would have been fitting for him to take a bite, for Twain was a man who loved to eat. Hot buttered biscuits and porterhouse steak were among his favorite foods.

Better yet, Twain once gave this piece of sage advice: "Never trust a man who has only one way to spell a word."

The Dogfather

James Mallis could only imagine what his new life would be like in the land of opportunity. The American dream was as wide and deep as the ocean he crossed to reach it.

According to oral history, he was born in the dirt-poor village of Voutiro in the Greek province of Evrytania, where the snows came every October and nobody saw the ground again until April. The villagers had to travel by mules down narrow mountainous paths.

Like other European immigrants looking to trade the old country for this brave new world, Mallis sought the prospects of a better life. There were no guarantees. He was unfamiliar with the language and the customs. Many immigrants could not make it in America and returned to their homelands.

Few would have ever believed this mysterious Greek man would wrap his arms around an all-American food and become the founding father of what is now the oldest restaurant in Macon, Georgia, and one of the oldest hot dog stands in the U.S.

(Then again, the earliest known reference to a hot dog came from a Greek guy. In the ninth century BC, Homer made reference to a "sausage" in his epic poem *The Odyssey*.)

So maybe it was predestination that Mallis would break ground, and the Nu-Way legacy would be passed down into the next century, through eighteen different Greek owners.

When Mallis sailed into New York Harbor in 1914, he was fascinated by the sights and sounds of the largest city in America. There were trolleys, horse-drawn carriages, and Model A automobiles on the streets. Women strolled through open markets and well-dressed men in hats stood reading

There is More than One Way to Spell Wiener

The view up Cotton Avenue (on right) in 1912. The ship's bell in front of the Commercial Savings Bank on the corner was taken from one of the first steamboats used on the nearby Ocmulgee River.
(Photo Courtesy of The Macon Telegraph)

their newspapers on every street corner. The approaching World War I was on everybody's mind.

Mallis found work as a dishwasher. Greek immigrants lacked the skills for most jobs, but some were able to find work mopping floors and cleaning tables in the restaurants and cafes. Mallis was intrigued with the hot dogs, which had gotten their name from the vendors at the Polo Grounds in New York City thirteen years earlier.

The Germans claim to have given birth to the hot dog in the fifteenth century in the city of Frankfurt, thus the name "frankfurter." The Austrians likewise contend it was a butcher from Coburg named Johann Georghehner, who traveled to Frankfurt two centuries later to promote the original wiener, which got its name from the city of Vienna, or "Wien."

Mallis was enamored with the idea of wrapping a "dachshund" sausage (named after the long, skinny dog) in a bun and making a meal out of it.

They had been sold on Coney Island in Brooklyn since 1871, when a butcher named Charles Feltman played matchmaker between a German sausage and an ordinary milk roll and sold an average of a hundred a day along the boardwalk.

The idea for the modern-day hot dog bun may have been introduced at the World's Fair in St. Louis in 1904, when a concessionaire named Anton Feuchtwanger grew weary of handing out gloves to his customers who bought sausages so they the would not burn their hands or get them greasy. So he had his brother-in-law, who was a baker, create a long, soft roll to cradle the sausage.

Twelve years later, Mallis hopped a train 900 miles south to Macon. He had a few friends and relatives in the Georgia city, which had a population of about 45,000 and was in the process of building the Terminal Station. Macon was on the cusp of being transformed into a major railroad transportation hub.

On February 27, 1916, Mallis opened a hot dog stand at 214-216 Cotton Avenue. On one side of him was Merkel's Bakery. On the other was Hodges & Geeslin Produce.

The location never changed, but the number later became 430 Cotton Avenue, where Nu-Way is still in operation today.

Mallis held his grand opening without much fanfare. It was only a few weeks after Nathan Handwerker opened Nathan's Famous Hot Dogs on Coney Island, which currently holds the distinction of being the oldest hog dog stand in America.

There were other hot dog stands in Macon at the time, but Mallis served his hot dogs with a twist. He wanted to differentiate himself from the others, so he took the chili sauce he had developed and slapped it over the hot dog when it was fresh off the grill.

The dozen ingredients for his special chili sauce were a closely guarded secret, so much that he reportedly would lock the kitchen doors while he was making it.

There is yet another deep, dark secret about James Mallis. Even though there was a "James Mallios" [sic] listed as living at the Edgerton Hotel on Broadway in the 1918 Macon City Directory, there are some who suspect James Mallis was not the real name of the Nu-Way founder.

The late George Andros, a Nu-Way co-owner from 1936-99, speculated Mallis may have actually been John Kokinos, who was listed as co-owner with Gus Psilopoulos in 1918. (The Greek translation of his name was "Red," which may further explain Nu-Way's traditional red-colored dogs, a Coney Island tradition.)

When Andros traveled back to Greece, he could find none of Mallis's descendants or relatives in any of the close-knit villages. It seems no one knew or had even heard of Demetrios Alexandros Malliotis.

Yet the name of James Mallis lives on with a star on his dressing-room door. He is a legend, and his name is associated with nearly every history account ever written about Nu-Way. He has been immortalized in magazine articles, brochures, and websites. His "new way" has endured for almost a century, closing in on 175 million hot dogs sold.

He was the dogfather.

(Above) The view down Cotton Avenue in the early 1900s. James Mallis would open his hot dog stand just past the triangular park on the right. (Photo Courtesy of The Macon Telegraph)

Anatomy of a
Nu-Way Weiner

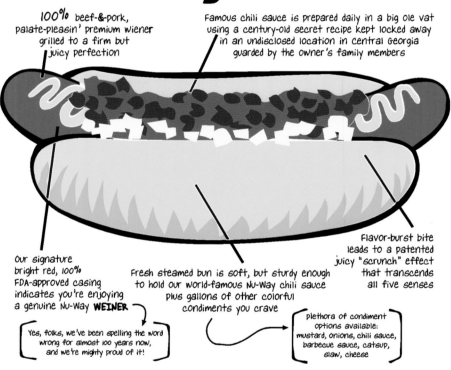

100% beef-&-pork, palate-pleasin' premium wiener grilled to a firm but juicy perfection

Famous chili sauce is prepared daily in a big ole vat using a century-old secret recipe kept locked away in an undisclosed location in central Georgia guarded by the owner's family members

Our signature bright red, 100% FDA-approved casing indicates you're enjoying a genuine Nu-Way **WEINER**

Fresh steamed bun is soft, but sturdy enough to hold our world-famous Nu-Way chili sauce plus gallons of other colorful condiments you crave

Flavor-burst bite leads to a patented juicy "scrunch" effect that transcends all five senses

Yes, folks, we've been spelling the word wrong for almost 100 years now, and we're mighty proud of it!

plethora of condiment options available: mustard, onions, chili sauce, barbecue sauce, catsup, slaw, cheese

(Photo courtesy of Nu-Way)

10

The Red State

OK, so it's red.

But not just any red.

It has been called everything from fire-engine red to lipstick red to candy-apple red. It could be a soft shade of ruby, with a splash of sunset.

(Just don't call those dogs Georgia Bulldog red. After all, Nu-Way is owned by a couple of well-red…er, well-*read* Georgia Tech graduates.)

The trademark red hot dogs have been a topic of conversation for years on the sidewalks of Macon. One of the original Nu-Way owners was Gus "Red" Psilopoulos. The builder of the famous neon sign on Cotton Avenue was named Red Davis.

Maybe it was destiny.

In keeping with its Coney Island roots, a Nu-Way hot dog is red. It is made up of a beef and pork weiner served on a steamed bun, topped off with an all-meat (beanless) chili, chopped onions, and mustard.

If you travel across the weiner nation, you'll find there are almost as many ways to prepare hot dogs as there are people in the world.

In Birmingham, you can get a hot dog served with sauerkraut, ground beef, and homemade sauce. In West Hollywood, California, it is possible to order tandem hot dogs on a flour tortilla, covered with chili and pastrami and wrapped up like a burrito.

In the Windy City of Chicago, where ketchup is taboo on hot dogs, they steam them and pile on the chopped onions, tomatoes, pickled peppers, dill spears, mustard and celery salt. In Tucson, you can find them wrapped in mesquite-smoked bacon, topped with freshly chopped tomatoes, onions, shredded cheese, red chili sauce, and even pinto beans.

In Kansas City, you can expect sauerkraut and Swiss cheese, minus the holes. Boston's famous Fenway frank is part of the required diet for Red Sox fans. They steam them and load them up with mustard, relish, ketchup, and chopped onions.

In New Jersey, you don't have to order fries because your potato dog will come with diced potatoes and brown mustard. In Seattle, they toast the buns and grill the dogs and top them off with cream cheese, grilled onions and even jalapeños.

And lest we forget Pittsburgh, home of the "Big O," The Original Hot Dog Shop, where they're smothered with cheese, bacon, and everything from relish to mustard, ketchup, pickles, onions, chili, mayonnaise, and sauerkraut.

Nu-Way co-owner Jim Cacavias remembers leaving his office one afternoon when two women walking down Cotton Avenue came up and introduced themselves. One of them was from Pittsburgh.

Jim was curious. "Well, what do you think of our hot dogs?" he asked.

"It was the best hot dog I've ever eaten," she said. "But I must admit it took me a while to get over the red."

The Nu-Way owners are accustomed to fielding questions about the red hot dogs. Their explanation?

"Red has always been the Nu-Way way," said Dermatas. "Hot dogs were originally called 'red hots' because of the red sausage weiner. There was a scare in the 1970s concerning the issue of red dye, but we follow all FDA guidelines and regulations. When you go to the grocery store, the hot dogs from Oscar Mayer or Ballpark are in a natural-color casing for aesthetics. You can also get red or orange. Most of the casings are synthetic. It's the only way to form the shape of the dog."

Said Cacavias, "For a while, hot dogs got a bad rap, so the food industry got away from the red. The manufacturers felt the heat from the public and decided to go to the clear, natural casings. People look at our red hot dogs and want to know what is in them, as if they were some lower form of meat. There is the perception we are trying to hide something with the red casing."

Once folks get past the red zone, the hot dogs are worth it.

They are grilled, not boiled, using a hamburger flipper with a brush of vegetable oil on a flat-iron grill.

"If you go to Coney Island, or any of the famous hot dog places, that's the way they do it," said Dermatas. "It's a beef-pork weiner, and they do it by feel and look."

Cacavias's father, John, had a saying: "The gas grill is your best friend."

"There's just something about it," said Dermatas. "It gets used so many times, it gives everything that seasoned taste."

The hot dogs are manufactured to withstand temperatures up to 400 degrees on a grill. Dermatas said most of the hot dogs bought at grocery stores are made to be boiled, not grilled.

Another key ingredient is the bun itself. It is steamed for three to four minutes in a gas bun warmer, true Coney Island style.

Nu-Way has a contract for its bread products through Flowers Foods in Savannah. At one time, Nu-Way used so much bread for its buns the Georgia Baking Company, owned by the Hobby family, was actually next to the Cotton Avenue Nu-Way.

In the early years, the hot dogs were made by the Thomas and Tucker families at T&T packaging on Seventh Street. It was a slaughter house, and a German-Austrian sausage maker who worked there helped develop the hot dog. The plant burned in 1971 and moved to Griffin, as the Thomas Packing Co. Nu-Way continued to have its special label hot dogs made there until that plant suffered a fire, too.

After several years of trying to find another manufacturer, Nu-Way settled on Kent Quality Foods in Grand Rapids, Michigan.

"We didn't have to find them; they came to us," said Dermatas. "That's all they do—make weiners for everybody. We have our own label. Their reputation is one of the best in the nation for safety in the way they gas-pack the weiner. That was a big issue for us. The consistency is much better, too. They make an awesome product."

It has nothing to do with the color of the hot dogs, but red is also a primary color in Nu-Way's color scheme.

When Cacavias was working as a consulting engineer in the 1980s and '90s, he helped open several Enmark gas and convenience stores. Enmark stood for "Energy Marketing," and the company hired a consultant to help with imaging as the stores opened along interstate highways.

"He suggested red and yellow as the company's colors because he said it was subliminal," said Jim. "Your eyes and your brain will automatically pick up red and yellow first. You are psychologically trained to pay attention to red and yellow traffic signals and signs. It is red first, and yellow second."

So when Jim returned in 1998, Nu-Way began to convert its color scheme from red, white and blue to red, yellow, and black.

When you operate a hot dog restaurant, red and yellow might have yet another subliminal meaning...especially when you're hungry.

"Ketchup and mustard," Jim said, laughing.

Pass the Napkins, Please

It starts with the chili.

On the grill line at the Nu-Way, it is considered one of the five major food groups.

It has enough bang and twang to cause a sensation. There is a hint of cinnamon, a dash of barbecue sauce to smooth it out and enough kick to jump-start a fleet of muscle cars.

The chili is the signature dish. It is such a staple that, if you order a "Nu-Way," they'll serve you a chili dog with mustard and onions. That's the definition of a "Nu-Way."

When James Mallis left the Big Apple for the Peach State, he was packing some high heat in his suitcase.

Coney Island may have been a hotbed for hot dogs, but it also boasted its share of places that could serve a mean bowl of chili.

Mallis took a weiner over here and piled on some chili over there, then pronounced them man and wife—the original big, fat Greek wedding.

His recipe for chili has remained basically unchanged over the years, with a few tweaks and refinements. Some of the tinkering has come out of necessity because the manufacturers of the different spices have changed over the years.

"It has a zing to it," said co-owner Spyros Dermatas. "It's spicy. It has a very strong profile."

The secret recipe is locked away in a vault and stored in the memory of those who have answered the higher calling to prepare it over the years. Often imitated, rarely duplicated.

"My dad used to say you can take any food product to a laboratory, and they can break it down for you," said co-owner Jim Cacavias. "They can tell

Chili dogs are the signature dish for generations of Nu-Way fans (Photo courtesy of Nu-Way)

you how much ground beef is in it and which spices were used. So you've got the recipe. But that's only the half of it. The other part is the procedure of when to add certain ingredients and how to cook it. The chili recipe is fairly easy. But why hasn't anybody been able to duplicate it? It's the methodology."

Longtime owners George Andros and Gus Lolos were credited with taking the original Mallis gem and elevating it to a new level. At one point in the 1920s, Nu-Way served its chili as "Mexican Style."

The restaurant uses chili peppers with varying degrees of smack and even has its own blend. Since the late 1940s, it has a long-standing relationship of buying all of its spices—from the black pepper to the oregano—from A. C. Legg, a packer in Alabama, south of Birmingham.

There are eleven spices in all and, yes, they've been spooning in some sweet barbecue sauce through four generations of cooks. There are also roasted and finely cut pork shoulders and hams tossed in for good measure.

SLAW DOG

July is National Hot Dog month, and July 4 is the biggest hot dog holiday of the year. According to the National Hot Dog and Sausage Council, Americans eat more than 150 million on that day alone.

So Jim Cacavias wasn't surprised when he picked up a Sunday edition of *The New York Times* on July 2, 2002, and noticed the big headline "High Spots in a Nation of Hot-Dog Heavens" in the food section.

But he almost fell out of his chair when he saw the accompanying story, which crowned Nu-Way as having the best slaw dog in America.

"Southerners have long understood that coleslaw makes a cooling counterpoint to spicy barbecue, and many of them have applied this approach to hot dogs," Paul Lukas wrote. "The acknowledged king of this particular hill is the Nu-Way Weiners in Macon, Ga., where the fresh homemade slaw is a popular topping on the shop's red-hots (which are literally bright red, making for a nice piece of visual flair)."

Cacavias, who was vacationing with his family, called his business partner in Macon.

"You won't believe it, we're in *The New York Times*!" he said.

"You've got to be kidding," said Dermatas.

But he wasn't. There it was in black and white, along with all the other news that's "fit to print." Dermatas drove to Kroger and bought every copy of the Sunday *Times*.

Cacavias could hardly wait to call his dad with the exciting news. John Cacavias was credited with coming up with the slaw recipe.

"It was special to me that he lived to see it [John died in 2004]," he said. "He would sit there in the mornings with cabbage and say 'let's try it this way' or 'let's try it that way.' He would add a little salt or a little sugar until he got it right. When we added some onions, he said, 'No onions!' "

If John is credited with coming up with the right combination for the blue-ribbon slaw, Chuck Gordon at least deserves an honorable mention for his persistence.

Gordon, who was manager of the Bloomfield Nu-Way, was a native New Yorker with a diverse background. He was a retired colonel who ended up at Robins Air Force Base. He met and married Georgia Mae Hill, who had worked at the Nu-Ways on Cotton and Houston avenues for more than thirty years.

"He kept telling us we had to have coleslaw, we had to have coleslaw," said Dermatas. "He said folks were coming in and calling him at Bloomfield. They were driving him crazy about wanting slaw dogs. So we caved in and said we would do it."

The decision also came in response to the competition. Johnny Vastakis, a former Nu-Way manager, had opened his own chain of thirteen hot-dog restaurants across Macon and Middle Georgia called Johnny V's. He offered slaw dogs on the menu.

John Cacavias was an excellent cook who had made slaw for the Moderna Cafe he and Nick Dermatas opened in Augusta in the 1950s. So he used fresh cabbage as his foundation, chopped it thin, and kept it simple. It was creamy, with no carrots or onions.

"The real secret is the high quality dressing," said Dermatas. "We use only one manufacturer for that, and we make the slaw in-house. The key is to keep it fresh. The thing about slaw is that, as soon as you mix it, it starts degrading. So

The New York Times voted the slaw dog as the top dog in the nation (Photo courtesy of Nu-Way)

we don't keep it for more than forty-eight hours. We tell our managers to flip the gallon jugs every six hours."

The slaw dog was rolled out in 1980 and is still going strong.

SCRAMBLED DOG

You have to drive ninety-five miles to Dinglewood Pharmacy in Columbus, Georgia, to dine on the original scrambled dog. And Macon's most famous hot dog restaurant can't even claim to be the first to serve it in its own city.

Roy Gandy opened a pool hall on Cherry Street in 1937, the same year Nu-Way unveiled its neon sign up the hill on Cotton Avenue. Legend has it Gandy traveled to Columbus to collect a debt from someone and came back with the recipe for a scrambled dog in his corner pocket.

But when the pool hall eventually closed, and its popular dish left with it, the appetite for scrambled dogs lingered. At the time, the Nu-Way menu offered a bowl of chili (with beans) with a side of oyster crackers, but there was enough customer demand in the 1980s to warrant adding a scrambled dog platter to the fare.

So now Nu-Way pours a bowl of chili with all those spices and two different kinds of Mexican-style beans over the top of an open-face hot dog, with a variety of toppings. And, oh yeah, don't forget the oyster crackers.

MEGA-BURGER

Can the place that lays claim to the "best weiner in town" offer hamburgers on the menu?

Well, there's no law against it.

But can a hot dog stand think outside the bun enough to create a hamburger that will make people forget they came in for a slaw dog and fries?

Over the years, Nu-Way began to diversify its menu, first out of necessity, then to remain competitive.

The Mega-Burger, a quarter-pound of ground beef with all the toppings, is served home style, with a waffle pattern, not thick and chewy. There is a method to its gladness. The bread is toasted on the griddle, then the mayonnaise is spread on the top and the ketchup on the bottom, because that's the way it has been

Customers asked for the scrambled dog and Nu-Way delivered. (Photo courtesy of Nu-Way)

Mega-Burger is still a "big boy" and "mega" is Greek for "large" (Photo courtesy of Nu-Way)

done for more than a generation. The lettuce and tomatoes are always placed on top of the burger.

Until the 1950s, a large hamburger on the Nu-Way menu was known as a "Big Boy Burger."

Apparently, no one realized Shoney's restaurants had already claimed the name "Big Boy" for its famous hamburgers. Rather than become involved in a legal battle, Nu-Way changed the name to "Mega-Burger." Mega is Greek for large.

BREAKFAST DISHES

In the late 1940s, Nu-Way began sneaking past the roosters every morning to offer a traditional breakfast fare.

It wasn't entirely by design that owners George and Harry Andros and Gus Lolos positioned themselves for a sunrise service. During the Depression, they often could not get hot dogs from the suppliers, so they sold egg sandwiches and grilled cheese sandwiches instead.

The experience Nick Dermatas and John Cacavias received from running diners in Augusta and Valdosta also contributed to opening the Nu-Way doors at dawn and helping Macon wake up and smell the coffee.

"When Nu-Way first started serving breakfast, we had glasses for the orange juice, thick china mugs for coffee cups, and real silverware," said Dermatas. "The birthplace of eating out for breakfast was the all-American diner. Breakfast was eaten at the counter. It was not ordered to-go. Wrapping an egg sandwich would have been something very foreign to them."

Locally, Krystal was the only fast-food competitor that offered breakfast in the 1960s. McDonald's and others followed.

The top-selling item on the Nu-Way breakfast menu is the bacon-and-egg sandwich. The second-most popular is a more traditional platter of two eggs with toast or biscuits, grits or fries, jelly, and butter.

There's nothing tricky about it.

"We crack the eggs on a flat gas grill," said Dermatas. "It's the same grill we cook the hamburgers on, so it gives it a different taste. When you use a gas grill, it makes the eggs fluffier than on an electric grill. And we use real eggs, not an egg substitute. You can cook sunny side up or over light. You can't do that with Egg Beaters."

Maconites have been waking up to Nu-Way for years (Photo courtesy of Nu-Way)

FAMOUS FLAKY ICE

It's just ice. There is no secret recipe locked away in a safe deposit box. It's just frozen water. There are no fancy gimmicks.

But wait. The ice...yes, the ice...almost has a cult following.

Folks don't just make pilgrimages to the Nu-Way for the dogs. They have to wash them down with a thirty-two-ounce tea, a forty-four-ounce Coca-Cola, or maybe a twenty-ounce pink lemonade.

Best of all, it's served over that "Famous Flaky Ice." The ice machine cranks it out with a slightly different texture than regular crushed ice.

And when they carry it out with them—long after lunch has been devoured—the flaky ice will spend the afternoon with them in that Styrofoam cup. Some days, it will even outlast them.

As far back as the 1980s, the ice had achieved enough notoriety the Nu-Way ownership determined it needed to have its own identity. Although the term "Famous Flaky Ice" was too generic to qualify for a trademark, a local advertising agency came up with a logo.

How many restaurants have a name for their ice?

Even the ice is famous at Nu-Way (Photo courtesy of Nu-Way)

Speaking the Language

Gimme two and a fry to stay! (Photo courtesy of Nu-Way)

Gimme two and a fry to go!

Two hot dogs "all the way" and a small order of French fries.

Gimme two without and a fry to go!

Two hot dogs without onions and a small order of French fries.

Gimme one of each and a fry to go!

One hot dog and one hamburger "all the way" and a small order of French fries.

Gimme one of each without and a fry to go!

One hot dog and one hamburger without onions and a small order of French fries.

Gimme two heavy chili to stay!

Two hot dogs "all the way" with heavy chili sauce.

Gimme a meg with cheese to go!

One Mega-Burger with cheese.

Gimme five, two, and three to go!

Five hot dogs "all the way," two hamburgers "all the way," and three small orders of French fries.

Gimme six "all the way," two plain, and three fries to go!

Six hot dogs "all the way," two hot dogs plain, and three small orders of French fries.

Gimme two to stay!

Two hot dogs "all the way" to stay.

Gimme a HLT no mayo to stay!

Ham, lettuce, and tomato sandwich on toasted white bread without the mayonnaise. (Comes with an order of small French fries.)

**Gimme two over-easy
with bacon and two cakes
on the side to stay!**

*Two eggs over-easy, with an order of
bacon, grits, white-buttered toast,
and two pancakes as a side order.
(No need to mention the grits and
white-buttered toast—they're
automatic.)*

**Gimme a double-scrambled loaded
and a large fry to stay!**

*Scrambled dog platter with two
weiners with mustard and onions
and a large order of French fries.
(Normally a scrambled dog platter
does not include mustard and
onions.)*

**Gimme a meg to stay—
make it "mega-super-size!"**

*One Mega-Burger with double
patties. (Comes with a small order
of French fries.)*

Gimme a dog house plain to go!

*Kids Dog House box with a plain
hot dog, one small order of French
fries, one lollipop and a Nu-Way
tattoo.*

**Gimme two mini-megs
with bacon to go!**

*Two two-ounce burgers with
lettuce, tomatoes, mayonnaise, and
ketchup with one strip of bacon.
(A "smaller" version of Mega-
Burger, but it does not come with
the small order of French fries.)*

Gimme two mini-malts to go!

*Two twelve-ounce cups of chocolate
malt. (Chocolate is the only flavor.)*

**Gimme one just ketchup
and a kiddie Coke to go!**

*One hot dog with ketchup only and
one twelve-ounce Coca-Cola.*

**Gimme a "3 for 2"without/with
slaw to go with a tea!**

*Three hot dogs without onions, add
coleslaw on top, one small order of
French fries and a thirty-two-ounce
cup of sweet iced tea. (This "3-for-
2" special is good only on Mondays,
Tuesdays, and Wednesdays, and
the third hot dog or hamburger
is free.)*

Breakfast

Hot & Hearty....*made to order! Start your day the* **Nu-Way!**

Toasted Sandwiches

Sausage & Egg Sandwich	2.89
Bacon & Egg Sandwich	2.79
Ham & Egg Sandwich	2.99
Egg Sandwich	1.89

Biscuits

Sausage & Egg Biscuit	1.89
Bacon & Egg Biscuit	1.79
Ham & Egg Biscuit	1.99
Egg Biscuit	1.49

Sausage Biscuit	1.49
Bacon Biscuit	1.39
Ham Biscuit	1.59
Plain Biscuit *butter & jelly*	.99

Platters

Two Eggs*	*toast or biscuit, grits or fries, jelly & butter*	2.99
One Egg*	*toast or biscuit, grits or fries, jelly & butter*	2.79
Three Pancakes *syrup & butter*		3.99

Side Orders

Order of Sausage *2 patties*	1.89
Order of Bacon *3 strips*	1.79
Order of Ham	1.99
Order of Country Ham	2.89
Order of Streak o'Lean	1.79

Order of Toast *butter & jelly*	.99
Bowl of Grits *10 oz.*	.99
Side Order of Two Eggs*	1.69
Tater Rounds	1.09

(breakfast items may vary by location)

Main Menu

Hot Dogs

Our famous grilled **Nu-Way Weiner**, *along with our mouth watering homemade chili sauce, combine to create one of America's truly original and unique hot dogs. Just remember that mustard, onions & chili sauce mean* **"All the Way"**

Hot Dog *"All the Way"*	1.79
Slaw Dog *our homemade cole slaw*	1.79
Cheese Dog *"All the Way"*	2.14
Chili-Slaw Dog	2.14
Chili-Cheese Slaw Dog *"All the Way"*	2.49
Chili-Bean Dog	2.39
Hot Dog *"plain"*	1.69

Hamburgers

Hamburger *"All the Way"*	1.79
Cheeseburger *"All the Way"*	2.14
Hamburger *"plain"*	1.69
MEGABURGER® *"A Meal in Itself"* *deluxe 1/4-pounder w/fries*	4.59
with bacon & cheese	6.33
Mega-Super-Size - double patty	5.98
with bacon & cheese	7.72
Chili-Cheese Meg *w/fries*	5.74
Mini-Meg	2.29

Sandwiches

Grilled Cheese	1.84
Patty Melt *w/fries*	4.59
Grilled Ham & Cheese *w/fries*	4.59
B.L.T. *w/fries*	4.39
Ham-Club Double Decker *w/fries*	5.89
Grilled Bacon & Cheese *w/fries*	4.39
Ham, Lettuce & Tomato *w/fries*	4.59

Platters

Scrambled Dog	*open faced hot dog platter loaded with chili w/beans*	4.19
Double Scrambled Dog	*same as above but w/two weiners*	4.98

Main Menu

Combos

Combo #1 *one hot dog or one hamburger, small fries & 20 oz drink* **4.97**

Combo #2 *two hot dogs or two hamburgers, small fries & 32 oz drink* **6.96**

Combo #3 - 3 for 2 Special
(mon. tue. and wed. only) **6.96**
three hotdogs or three hamburgers, or any combination w/ small fries & 32 oz drink

Kids Dog House *one hotdog or hamburger or grilled cheese or four chicken nuggets w/ small fries & 12 oz drink* **3.99**

Chicken and fish

Chicken Sandwich	**2.99**
Chicken Nuggets *crispy & tender fritters*	
small (8) **2.59** large (12) **3.79**	
Tuna Salad Sandwich *w/ let. & tom.*	**2.99**
Fish Sandwich *4 oz flounder filet*	**2.99**

Side Items

French Fries	*small* **1.59**	*large* **2.34**
Chili Fries	*small* **2.39**	*large* **3.09**
Chili-Cheese Fries *small* **2.79**		*large* **3.49**
Onion Rings *home-style battered*		
	small **1.79**	*large* **2.59**
LAYS Potato Chips *(classic, baked or bbq)* **1.24**		
Chili w/ Beans		
10 oz bowl **2.29** *20 oz cup* **3.99** *32 oz quart* **5.99**		
Cole Slaw		
4 oz **.99** *10 oz* **2.09** *32 oz quart* **5.99**		
		gallon **22.99**
Pickles	*4 oz* **.89**	*10 oz* **1.89**

* These items cooked to order.

FOOD ADVISORY: Consuming raw or undercooked foods such as meat, poultry, fish, shellfish and eggs may increase your risk of food borne illness.

Drinks & Desserts

Drinks

*Our **Famous Flaky Ice** in our soft drinks "Tops Them All"!*

Coca-Cola Classic, Sprite, Diet Coke, Fanta Orange, Dr. Pepper, Hi-C Pink Lemonade

20 oz **1.59**   *32 oz* **1.79**   *44 oz* **1.99**

Iced Tea   *20 oz* **1.59**   *32 oz* **1.79**   *44 oz* **1.99**
gallon without ice **4.99**

Coffee	*12 oz* **.89**	*20 oz* **1.29**
Hot Chocolate	*12 oz* **.89**	*20 oz* **1.29**
Sanka	*12 oz* **.89**	*20 oz* **1.29**

Orange Juice	*10 oz* **1.29**
Kiddie Soft Drink	*12 oz* **1.39**

Chocolate Malt *delicious & triple-thick*
20 oz **2.39**   *32 oz* **3.49**   *44 oz* **4.59**

Desserts

Hot Apple Turnover	**1.19**
Chocolate Mini-Malt	*12 oz* **1.69**
Ice Cream *cup or sugar cone chocolate, vanilla, strawberry, rainbow sherbert, and other flavors*	
single **1.99** *double* **2.99**	

(at select locations)

All prices are subject to change without notice. Thank you.

**Top, left to right: George Andros, Harry Andros
Bottom, left to right: Nick Dermatas, John Cacavias** (Photos courtesy of Nu-Way)

30

The Fab Four

If there was a hot dog hall of fame, or a Mount Rushmore for Mega-Burgers, the Fab Four would have been inducted as members of the first class.

George Andros.

Harry Andros.

Nick Dermatas.

John Cacavias.

Their names evoke a kind of reverence at Nu-Way, like Greek gods who took small, careful steps and giant leaps of faith. They stirred their chili in the morning and quietly counted their money at night. They stood over a hot grill on Cherry Street and gave their employees rides home from Houston Avenue at closing time.

They loved and were loved.

George and Harry Andros were stepbrothers whose careers at Nu-Way spanned parts of eight different decades. They held every job there was, from curb boy to waiter to chief cooks and bottle washers. George became an owner in 1936, the year before the famous neon sign went up in lights, and Harry became a partner ten years later. Together, they remained as owners until 1999.

Nick Dermatas and John Cacavias were brothers-in-law. They married sisters in the Andros family and eventually joined the ownership circle. Nick was a tireless worker whose charming personality made him popular with all his employees. John was an intellect who served on secret missions with the Army during World War II. He will forever be known as the brains behind the coleslaw recipe that led the way for Nu-Way to be voted "best slaw dog in America" by the *New York Times* in 2002. Their sons, Spyros Dermatas and Jim Cacavias, carry on their legacy as co-owners today.

George Andros came to America when he was fourteen years old in 1929 to work for his father, James Andros, who had immigrated to find work and provide for his family back in Greece. George's mother had died when he was young, and his father re-married.

He would tell the story about how he spent eleven days on a French ocean liner. When he arrived in New York Harbor, he didn't speak English. The people in the immigration office helped him board a train headed south and offered him something to eat. He declined, thinking he would be in Macon by suppertime. It was a good thing his father ran a restaurant called the Palace of Sweets, less than a block from Terminal Station. He arrived at the train station thirty-three hours later. He was starved.

George worked for his father for a few years, then took a second job at the Nu-Way as a curb boy. His first day on the job was March 17, 1929. He would take orders from the cars, run back and place the order, then return with the hot dogs.

He would also take orders from businessmen and secretaries downtown. Sometimes the lines would wrap all the way around to Poplar Street, and it was not unusual for Nu-Way to sell 2,000 hot dogs at lunch time.

"During the Depression, we gave away more hot dogs than we sold," he once said in an interview." People would see the hot dogs cooking in the window and come up to you and beg you for something to eat."

He worked his way up the ladder until 1936 when he bought half-interest in Nu-Way. His name would remain on the ownership list for the next sixty-three years.

He was clever and diplomatic enough to convince business partner Gus Lolos to agree to purchase the neon sign by telling him he was the chef depicted at the top of the sign. (Gus was flattered and bought into the idea.) George was smart enough to save money to go to college and study to become an electrical engineer. He enrolled in the Coyne Electrical School in Chicago and joined the Navy during World War II, where he was an engineering technician aboard the USS *Alabama*.

"When I was young, I was amazed at how meticulous he was," said Jim Cacavias. "He was always taking things apart, identifying the Achilles heel, then finding the solution and beefing it up. He could put a piece of equipment back into service that was better than what the manufacturer had made."

Spyros Dermatas remembers his uncle as being resourceful. He would rarely throw anything away. He didn't believe in a disposable society. He was recycling before recycling was cool.

"It was the way he was brought up," said Spyros. "He lived through the Depression. If we had a toaster come in from one of the restaurants that wasn't working, he would take it to a workbench in the back and take it apart."

George was successful in expanding the menu and remodeling the store, adding the first booths. He also pioneered the growth of Nu-Way, opening a second restaurant located on Cherry Street in May 1948.

Harry was six years younger than his stepbrother and joined him as a waiter in 1941. He, too, arrived in the U.S. with no English skills. Even though Harry was seventeen years old, George enrolled him at the Whittle School, a grammar school at the foot of Coleman Hill in downtown Macon. The other students teased him because he was so much older.

When he finally did learn to speak English, folks could hardly get him to stop talking.

"While Uncle George was a methodical thinker and a listener, Uncle Harry would just speak his mind," said Spyros. "They were both great restaurateurs and entrepreneurs."

They made a great team. When George went into the Navy, Harry signed up for the Army. Gus Lolos, the third partner, was too old to join the military so he stayed behind in Macon to hold down the fort. When the Andros brothers returned, they suddenly had three people running a tiny thirty-nine-seat restaurant, so they opened the Cherry Street location.

Nick Dermatas and John Cacavias grew up in the same part of Greece in villages only four miles apart. John was born in 1920, and Nick a year later. They both came to America in 1938, but their paths did not cross until they married sisters. Nick married Zoe Andros in 1951. John took Tasia Andros for his bride the following year.

Nick's mother died when he was two years old. His father never came to America. Nick boarded a freighter from Greece to Venice, Italy, and then to the U.S. He traveled with his friend and neighbor, Gus Priovolos, who was John's cousin. (Gus later became a well-known maître d' at the Waldorf-Astoria in New York, where he got to know a number of movie stars and other celebrities. There is a plaque honoring his thirty years of service near the coatroom at the hotel.)

Nick traveled on to Washington, D.C., where an uncle ran a popular tavern and gave him a job as a dishwasher. Nick stayed with the family in Arlington, Virginia, where his uncle's five daughters all treated him like a brother.

After serving in the Army from 1941-45 and marrying into the Andros family, Nick migrated to Macon in 1951, where he began as a waiter at the Nu-Way. John married and joined Nick in Macon in 1952, starting off as a grill man.

Together, they left Macon for a few years to venture out on their own. They opened The Moderna Cafe in Augusta, then sold it and went to Valdosta and opened the King's Grill downtown, which is still in operation today under different ownership. (George Andros had also opened a diner in Albany called The Quickie Shop, and then sold it to some cousins.)

By 1958, Nick had bought out Lolos, who owned half the company, then sold half of his share to John. They joined George and Harry Andros and each owned one-quarter of the business.

Nick was a popular boss because he was amicable. He was mild-mannered and got along with people. Everybody called him "Chief." It was a term of endearment.

"My father was more of a worker than an office type," said Spyros. "He hated to do the books. He didn't even have a checkbook. When it was time to pay the bills, he would walk to the different offices downtown and pay cash.

"He would roll up his sleeves and make sure things were right in the kitchen versus trying to sit there and balance a checkbook. He cooked the chili. It was his pride."

Nick didn't get his driver's license until 1966, when he was forty-five years old. He would catch the bus or rely on others to give him rides. He was also a sharp dresser who enjoyed joking around. Columnist Art Buchwald was his favorite writer, and he would rush home at night so he could catch his idol, Johnny Carson, on late-night television.

He died of a massive heart attack in August 1974. It was a Sunday night, and he had gone to Harry Andros's house to play cards. He wasn't much of a card-player, but he enjoyed hanging out with the guys, drinking coffee, and watching TV. He was reaching to put down his coffee cup when he collapsed.

John Cacavias came to America against his family's wishes. His mother and two brothers tried to convince him to stay in Greece, but he traveled to the U.S. to meet his father, who was working at a restaurant in the Virginia suburbs of Washington, D.C. John got a job there washing dishes. He would send some of his money back to Greece to help put his older brother through medical school.

When World War II broke out, he spent four years as an Army paratrooper with the Office of Strategic Services (OSS) on highly classified secret missions in Italy, Greece, Yugoslavia, and North Africa.

"My dad never could talk about it much because he was under oath not to discuss the missions for fifty years," said Jim Cacavias.

The OSS was created to conduct espionage activities behind enemy lines during World War II and led to the creation of the Central Intelligence Agency (CIA).

His pet name for his co-workers was "Jackson." He called everybody "Jackson." It was a holdover from his Army days.

John took another top secret to his grave.

He was responsible for creating the recipe for Nu-Way's delicious, creamy coleslaw, which earned the title of America's top slaw dog from *The New York Times*.

Some of the Greek Nu-Way family at Baconsfield Park in April 1953. Front row: (L-R) Harry P. Andros, Harry J. Andros, John Cacavias, George Andros, Nick Dermatas. Back row: Jimmy P. Andros, John Demos, James Anthony Chickas (Photo courtesy of Nu-Way)

Chronology of Nu-Way Owners

1916–1918

James Mallis

(Gus Psilopoulos starts as a clerk/waiter in 1917.)

1918–1922

John Kokinos and Gus Psilopoulos

(John N. Dermatas starts as a clerk/waiter in 1920. Tony Tsiklistas starts as a grill man in 1922.)

1922–1924

John N. Dermatas and
 Tony Tsiklistas

(Nick Komatas starts as a clerk/waiter in 1923.)

1924–1926

Tony Tsiklistas and Nick Komatas

(Gus Cacavias starts as a clerk/waiter in 1924.)

1926–1927

Tony Tsiklistas and Gus Cacavias

(Gus Baches starts as a cook in 1926.)

1927–1929

Tony Tsiklistas and Gus Baches

(George Andros starts as a part-time waiter in 1929. Nick Gioldas starts as a clerk/waiter in 1929.)

→

Chronology of Nu-Way Owners (continued)

Tony Tsiklistas (Photo courtesy of Nu-Way)

1929–1932
Tony Tsiklistas and Nick Gioldas
(Gus Lolos starts as a clerk/waiter in 1932.)

1932–1935
Nick Gioldas and Gus Lolos
(George Canoutas starts as a clerk/waiter in 1934.)

1935–1936
Gus Lolos and George Canoutas

1936–1945
Gus Lolos and George Andros
(Harry Andros starts as a waiter in 1941.)

1945–1958
Gus Lolos, George Andros, and
   Harry Andros
(Nick Dermatas starts as a waiter in 1951. John Cacavias starts as a grill man in 1952.)

1958–1974
George Andros, Harry Andros,
   Nick Dermatas, and John Cacavias

1974–1999
George Andros, Harry Andros,
   John Cacavias, and Zoe Dermatas

1999–Present
James Cacavias and Spyros Dermatas

(Third from left) John N. Dermatas in front of the old church bell tower in the village of Mikro Horio, Greece, 1959.
(Photo courtesy of Nu-Way)

Cousins Spyros Dermatas and Jim Cacavias have been co-owners of Nu-Way since 1999 (Photo by Ed Grisamore)

You Can Go Home Again

When he was a youngster, Jim Cacavias asked his father for an allowance. "I should get an allowance," he said. "All my friends get one."

"An allowance?" said John Cacavias. "Are you kidding me? If you don't work, you don't get paid."

That was the law of the land in the Cacavias and Dermatas households, along with others in the Greek community. A strong work ethic was encouraged and put into practice.

The families lived just two streets apart in the Riverside Park subdivision in Macon. And Jim and Spyros both started their Nu-Way careers at the restaurant on Houston Avenue, where their fathers were co-managers.

Spyros was twelve and Jim was nine when the first-cousins clocked in for the first time.

"It didn't matter if it was making French fries, pouring drinks, or sweeping the floor," said Spyros. "It was an adventure."

Jim spent his first day on the job pulling buns out of the steamer and stuffing weiners inside them for fifty cents a day. It was a labor of love.

Although Nu-Way's ownership followed a Greek pedigree from the beginning, there was no orchestrated family effort to groom either Jim or Spyros to follow in their fathers' footsteps.

In fact, it was quite the opposite.

"Our families encouraged us to pursue other fields, like engineering or law," said Spyros. "My mother wanted me to go into medicine, but I couldn't stand the sight of blood."

Jim had always loved building things as a child. He knew being an engineer was his life's calling the moment the bulldozers and concrete machines arrived a few blocks from his home in the mid-1960s, and construction on I-75 began in Macon. He and Spyros would ride their bikes to the end of the Avenue of Pines and sit on the hill and watch the earth movers.

"Every day, I watched them building that bridge across the interstate at Riverview Road," he said. "I was in awe."

Spyros and Jim both attended Mount de Sales Academy, a private, Catholic school and the oldest school in Macon. Spyros graduated in 1972 and enrolled at Georgia Tech as an architect major.

He later switched to industrial management after his father, Nick Dermatas, died of a heart attack in August 1974, a month before Spyros was to begin his junior year at Tech.

"My three uncles—George, Harry, and John—took me aside," he said. "Our families were all so close. They told me not to worry about the business. They said for me to go back to school in September, finish at Georgia Tech, and then see about my future."

Georgia Governor Nathan Deal with Cacavias and Dermatas at the annual Taste of Macon in Atlanta
(Photo courtesy of Nu-Way)

He convinced Jim to follow him to Georgia Tech. And he had big plans for the two of them to return to Macon after they completed their studies and take over the family business.

"Spyros used to tell me, 'I'll study management and come back and run 'em. And you study engineering and come back and open 'em up,'" Jim said.

Spyros graduated in 1976 and contemplated going to law school or business school. Instead, he came home to Nu-Way because of his deep loyalty to the family business.

He managed the store on Houston Avenue for a year and then transferred to Cotton Avenue as manager. He and his wife, Emily, stayed in Macon and raised their family.

"I had fraternity brothers who went on to work for big companies in places like New York, Cincinnati, and California," he said. "So, in a sense I was disappointed to go back to Macon. I wasn't jealous of them. I just envied the opportunity and experience of going somewhere else. But I don't have any regrets."

Jim graduated from Tech in 1979 and pursued his dream as a civil engineer, working in Macon, Savannah, and Columbia, S.C. He also did structural and environmental engineering. In Savannah, he worked with the port authority. In Columbia, he did mostly private development and owned a private consulting engineering firm.

In fourteen years, he assisted in the development of sixty restaurants for clients in three states—Georgia, South Carolina, and North Carolina.

He drank every drop of experience. In a sense, he considered himself a "spy," just like his father was in World War II.

"I was always interested in how others built them, and how and where they developed them," he said.

There were times when Jim thought of returning home to apply his knowledge and experience to the family business. But he never got the call from his father until 1998. At that point, Jim figured it was probably too late. He and his wife, Paula, and their two children, were settled in Columbia.

"I had my own business, I was making good money and I loved what I was doing," he said. "I could not see moving my family to Macon. So I told my dad no."

John Cacavias would ask his son again, with the same results. After John asked a third time, Jim had a sleepless night.

"I stayed up all night thinking about it," he said. "My dad had always taught me to set goals that were attainable—not too high or too low, then move on to the next goal. And I thought about all the goals I had set for myself. I had gotten my college degree, professional licenses, and owned my own business. Then I realized I had reached every goal except the first one. It was when Spyros had said, 'I'll study management and come back and run 'em. And you study engineering and come back and open 'em up.' "

So he sold his consulting engineering firm and returned to those deep roots. His father was ecstatic. Spyros was ecstatic. Each would bring their own strengths and talents to the operation.

On April 30, 1998, on the evening before Jim's first day back at Nu-Way, his mother prepared a large, Greek meal.

"Then my father dropped two big bombs on me," Jim said. "He congratulated me for being a third-generation owner. He had never told me that my grandfather, Gus Cacavias, had been an owner (in 1926–1927). He said he had not wanted to influence my decision to come back."

Then John Cacavias told his son that the next day, May 1, would mark his fortieth anniversary with Nu-Way. He had started on May 1, 1958.

"That's it for me," he said. "I've put in my forty years. It's all yours."

May 1 had always been a special day for John and Tasia Cacavias. The first day of May was part of an annual Greek festival celebrating flowers.

"My dad was an avid gardener, and he would always bring Mom flowers every May 1," said Jim. "And Mom would sing this Greek song, 'Proto Maya' about the first day of May."

On another May 1, in 2004, John Cacavias passed away, surrounded by his loving family.

Jim Cacavias is presented the keys to Nu-Way by his father, John, in 1998 (Photo courtesy of Nu-Way)

The front of the Cotton Avenue Nu-Way in the 1940s (Photo courtesy of Nu-Way)

The Queen and Her Court

George Andros used to call her "Mana." That's Greek for "mother."

The headquarters on Cotton Avenue is the mother ship, a place so revered and beloved the floors have had to be replaced four times.

It's almost impossible not to wax nostalgic when you walk in the door and take a seat at one of the booths along the wall or vintage stools at the counter.

"There's just something comforting about a place that doesn't change," said loyal patron Steve Wilson. "It's a place where you can always go back. It's the same as it always has been and probably always will be."

Some claim the food even tastes better at Nu-Way No. 1, which has sold hot dogs along Cotton Avenue for almost a century.

Wilson is a local attorney whose office is just around the corner. He eats at Nu-Way so often he usually doesn't even have to order. They know his favorite is the Mega-Burger with bacon and cheese.

But, on a busy Thursday lunch break, he decided to celebrate by plucking a double scrambled dog off the menu.

"Look at that," he said, lacing it with mustard. "That's a work of art. I'm not even going to eat it. I'm just going to look at it."

Perhaps no other place in Macon is more of a melting pot, and it has nothing to do with the cooking. On any given weekday, you will find bankers and attorneys sharing the same lunch counter with blue-collar laborers and drifters off the street. Preachers, teachers, policemen, sanitation workers, college students, secretaries, and starving artists all come through the door to break bread.

"It goes from A to Z," said co-owner Spyros Dermatas.

"When people come in the office and ask who our customers are we tell them everybody from the street workers to the mayor," said co-owner Jim Cacavias.

Wilson savors the lunch-time banter. It has its own personality.

"I love coming in here and cutting up with the employees," he said. "They welcome you with a smile and call you by name."

The Cotton Avenue Nu-Way is surrounded by history. Just a few foot-long hot dogs outside the front door is the majestic City Auditorium, built in 1925. It has a copper dome measuring 152 feet in diameter, making it one of the largest of its kind in the world. The two largest funerals in city history—for boxer W. L. "Young" Stribling and singer Otis Redding—were both held at the auditorium, as was the local filming of Oprah Winfrey's television show in November 2007.

Cotton Avenue was named for the cotton wagons that used to roll down the gentle slope to load the river barges. To the southwest along Cotton is Macon's

The scene inside Nu-Way on Cotton Avenue in 1948 (Photo courtesy of Nu-Way)

City Hall, which briefly served as the Georgia state capital during the Civil War from November 18, 1864, to March 11, 1865.

Up the hill along Cotton are the former studios of Capricorn Records, which helped make Macon the epicenter of Southern rock 'n roll in the 1960s and '70s, with such acts as the Allman Brothers, Wet Willie, and the Marshall Tucker Band.

For thirty-two years, it was the only Nu-Way in town. A second location opened near the foot of Cherry Street on May 12, 1948. The Cherry Street restaurant was damaged by a fire that began in the building next door in 1968 and did not re-open.

The first suburban store was built on Houston Avenue in 1962, bringing with it Macon's first drive-thru window. It closed on December 31, 2010.

A second suburban restaurant opened at Napier Square on Hillcrest Boulevard on May 31, 1968, and still another at the crossroads of Bloomfield and Rocky Creek roads on August 20, 1969, exactly one month to the day after the *Apollo 11* moon landing.

Nu-Way's first franchise, at the Stantom Plaza on Watson Boulevard, opened in February 1969. Of the six other franchises, only two remain in business—at Five Points in Fort Valley (1972) and Russell Parkway (2000) in Warner Robins.

(Franchises on Gresham Road in Atlanta, East Johnston Street in Forsyth, North Davis Drive in Warner Robins, North Center Street in Thomaston, and Macon Road in Perry are no longer in operation.)

Each of the other eight restaurants revolve around Cotton Avenue, like planets orbiting the sun. Cotton is the location of Nu-Way's front office, and its central kitchen and warehouse.

They may serve the same food at the same prices, but they are anything but carbon copies.

"From downtown to Bloomfield to Napier Square to Warner Robins and east Macon, each store has developed a culture of its own within the neighborhood," said Dermatas. "They have taken on the identity and personality of the people who eat there. We didn't hire from other restaurants. We grew from within. Our employees have been homegrown products who started out washing dishes, then moved up to grill worker, waitress, and then manager."

In some cases, the demographics of the neighborhoods have changed, and the restaurants have had to change with them. In still other cases, the surrounding businesses closed up around them—grocery stores, laundries, drug stores, and retail shops.

But Nu-Way has hung around—no longer just a place to eat and run, but a destination.

Having grown up in a succession of Greek ownership, Cacavias always knew that. But it wasn't until he returned home in 1998, after eighteen years working as a consulting engineer, that he was able to fully understand it.

"I never realized what a cult following this place has," he said. "To come back and hear all the stories made me appreciate it even more. It was very humbling. Nu-Way is still very popular with people. The passion is amazing."

BACONSFIELD

It is 6:30 A.M. The sun has barely lifted its head off its pillow, and the crows are starting to arrive at Nu-Way No. 5.

They could be called roosters—they sometimes get there before the doors open—but manager Diana Hunter calls them "crows."

"They're always picking on things, just like a crow," she said, laughing.

Bennie Ogletree is a founding member of the crows. He was walking on the floors at the Baconsfield Nu-Way before just about anyone else. As a teenager in the early 1970s, he worked for his father's concrete business, and they poured the foundation.

"I helped build this place," he said, proudly. "And I've been coming here ever since. It's part of my routine every morning. I love to meet people. It's like a network."

Arthur Meadows is another card-carrying member of a fraternity of men who gather by the dawn's early light and solve the problems of the world over grits and coffee. He works across the river at Macon Occupational Medicine, and he will show up to "jump start my brain" over scrambled eggs and some of that Baconsfield bacon.

"We talk about everything from sports, religion, politics to what's in the newspaper," he said.

By mid-morning, the Baconsfield Nu-Way is just warming up. It may be store No. 5 on the roll call, but it is No. 1 in sales.

Nu-Way on Cotton Avenue as it looks today (Photo by Walter Elliott Photography)

Location. Location. Location. It means everything. Baconsfield is just a soft lob from I-16 and at the confluence of two major roads. It is fronted across the parking lot by Emery Highway and flanked by a stretch of Gray Highway that is called North Avenue, across from the Baconsfield Shopping Center. It also probably doesn't hurt that it is tucked right behind the popular Krispy Kreme Doughnuts.

No. 5 is where Fort Hill, East Macon, downtown, and Shirley Hills get together. Folks come down from Gray, and over from Laurens, Twiggs, and Wilkinson counties. Before the Brown & Williamson plant closed in 2004, workers on the graveyard shift would often stop by for chili dogs between 7 and 9 in the morning. At lunchtime, the line sometimes stretches from the counter to the door.

Baconsfield has withstood a series of challenges since it opened in 1972. Within a few years, a McDonald's opened across the street on North Avenue.

The Baconsfield Nu-Way is the company's No. 1 store in volume (Photo by Walter Elliott Photography)

"I remember my dad thinking it was the end of the world," said Dermatas. "He thought McDonald's was going to kill us, that we were going to go bankrupt. And we did feel the pinch for about six or eight months. But what we found out was that the competition actually brought more traffic. The more the merrier."

Another test was the "backward" drive-thru. Motorists wanting to use the window service must travel up Wilson Street. If they are alone in the car, they must handle their transactions by reaching across the passenger seat.

Long arms help. Employees at Baconsfield have seen frustrated drivers have to put their cars in park, get out and walk around to the window. To make it easier, if the line of cars gets long, Hunter will often send one of her employees outside to take orders from car to car during rush hour.

Finally, the Baconsfield store survived a revolution, of sorts, when the lunch counter was removed in the late 1980s.

Bennie Ogletree, right, and Arthur Meadows, are two of Baconsfield's early-morning "crows" (Photo by Ed Grisamore)

"We were trying to make it self-service," said Dermatas. "With the counter, the customers would come and stay a long time. I can remember Jim Peacock, our manager at the time, called and asked me to come over. The employees were scared of the customers. A couple of customers had slung their trays on the trash receptacle bin out of disgust. They had really been spoiled over here, but we did go ahead and change it anyway."

BLOOMFIELD

Harry and Ginny Davis were practically raised on Nu-Ways. So it should come as no surprise that you can find them at Bloomfield almost every day for breakfast, and sometimes they'll even come back for lunch or supper.

One reason for their loyalty is because they have followed manager Charlene Davis to every store she has worked—from Napier to Houston Avenue to Bloomfield. She makes them feel like family, and that's important to them. Their lives have been touched in some way by almost every Nu-Way in the city.

When Harry was a student at Dudley Hughes Vocational School in the mid-1960s, he had a teacher named Steve Graves, a retired Navy officer, who would take the class down the street to an electrical shop near Cotton Avenue.

"He would send us over for Nu-Ways at lunch," said Harry. "I would get hot dogs all the way, and I remember he would always order a hot dog and a hamburger. And when some of the boys in the class didn't have money, he would buy their lunch for them."

Harry is retired from Georgia Power, and Ginny is also retired after cleaning houses for a living. They have a son and a nephew who live out-of-state and will sometimes make Nu-Way their first stop when they come home to Macon.

Bloomfield opened in 1969, and was the sixth store overall. It carries the designation of store No. 2 after Cherry Street did not reopen in 1968.

It was tucked away in a shopping center, which at one time had a Colonial Grocery Store. As the businesses and neighborhoods around it have been in transition, No. 2 has managed to endure some rocky times along Rocky Creek.

"It has had its ups and downs since the glory days of the 1970s," said Dermatas. "We had to be patient with it. There was the road construction on both Rocky Creek and Bloomfield. It was touch-and-go for a while. We didn't

Harry and Ginny Davis are among the loyal diners at Nu-Way's Bloomfield restaurant (Photo by Ed Grisamore)

know if we should sign another lease or try to get closer to the mall. There were just so many issues."

But the restaurant has seen a resurgence since the Houston Avenue restaurant closed on December 31, 2010. The stores were just four miles apart, and Bloomfield has inherited many of the longtime Houston Avenue patrons. Davis was general manager of both stores before Houston closed.

And, if cleanliness is next to godliness, Bloomfield is a deity, of sorts. The store has received four "Golden Spatula" awards for excellent health ratings from local television station WMAZ-TV.

Napier Square has been a midtown dining icon since the 1960s (Photo by Walter Elliott Photography)

NAPIER SQUARE

Sometimes you want to go where everybody knows your name.

And they're always glad you came.

A group of men has been holding court at the Napier Square Nu-Way for years, transforming the dining counter into one of midtown's most popular think tanks.

They convene around the counter about the middle of the morning. Sometimes they don't budge until the middle of the afternoon. There's a bit of territorial rights, too. They have their favorite stools, and they guard them like pews in a church.

The regulars at Napier Square sometimes claim their place at the counter like pews in a church (Photo by Ed Grisamore)

'There wasn't much out here when we opened' says Northside manager Diana Bailey.
The restaurant now ranks third in sales among Nu-Way's stores (Photo courtesy of Nu-Way)

"They have their regular seats and, if you sit in their regular seat, they will sit right next to you until you leave," said manager Makeia Brown. "They love the interaction at the counter, carrying on with us and talking with each other."

Unlike Baconsfield, where the lunch counter was removed and replaced with self-service ordering, management kept the status quo at Napier Square. It is part of what makes it special.

"It's one of our unique locations because the neighborhood accepts it so much," said Cacavias. "They are in here every day. They sit at the counter and socialize. Even though there is some crime in the surrounding areas, this store never gets broken into. These guys look after it like it's their own kitchen."

The shopping center that surrounds it, which was developed in the early 1960s, once was home to a Piggly Wiggly grocery and other stores. Most of those businesses are long gone, but there are still industrial parks in the area, as well as plenty of traffic on Napier Avenue, a major artery running from near the Mercer University campus downtown and the affluent north Macon suburbs.

NORTHSIDE

It was a giant leap of faith when Nu-Way stretched its kingdom to the northern 'burbs. The visionaries said growth was coming. The optimists said it was just a matter of time.

The old V. C. & L. Road was being paved and renamed Northside Drive. Shopping centers and apartment complexes were in the plans.

But one needed faith…and a long-range telescope.

"There wasn't much out here when we first opened," said Diana Bailey, now the manager at Northside. "We used to sit there at the cash register in the mornings and watch the deer play in the parking lot. We'd only have to cook four or five strips of bacon and had $15 in the register. We knew Mr. George (Andros) was downtown worrying if business was ever going to pick up."

Red hot dogs weren't the only red item at Northside. The store was swimming in red ink, losing money for its first three years of operation.

"It was a major decision on our part," said Dermatas. "We had signed a five-year lease with a five-year option, and we thought we had made a mistake. The volume just wasn't there. But, within a few more years, it exploded."

Businesses started moving in and, even though many later left the neighborhood, Nu-Way could finally see the forest through the trees at the corner of Forest Hill. Northside Drive was eventually widened for the 2.5-mile stretch from Riverside Drive to Wesleyan Drive.

Although the Northside Nu-Way has positioned itself in a strategic location in north Macon, it owes a huge measure of its success to Bailey, who has been with the company for thirty-three years, most of them at Northside.

Half of Nu-Way's current management team trained under her. Her store ranks third in volume behind Baconsfield and Zebulon.

"Nobody can touch her," said Dermatas. "She has a knack for the business. She was born to do what she's doing."

ZEBULON

When he was four years old, Mac Garvin watched the adorable movie *Babe* on video, then made a declaration to his father, Ken, on the way home from his grandparents' house.

He said he was never going to eat anything that comes from a pig. Not ham. Not bacon. Not…

"What about hot dogs?" asked Ken.

"Hot dogs don't come from pigs, Dad," Mac insisted. "They come from Nu-Way."

Nu-Ways have been a part of Mac's life since the day he was born on Groundhog's Day in 2001. His father used to walk down to Nu-Way for lunch when he was a student at Mount de Sales Academy. And while Paige Garvin was in the middle of her twenty-hour labor with Mac at The Medical Center of Central Georgia, Ken strolled down to the Nu-Way for a slaw dog.

"When he came back, the labor and delivery room smelled like Nu-Way," said Paige. "It was probably the first thing Mac smelled when he was born."

Ken and Mac still enjoy a father-and-son tradition of going to lunch together a couple of Saturdays each month at the Nu-Way on Zebulon Road. Mac usually orders the kid's meal. Ken gets the two hot dogs "all the way."

The Zebulon store, located in the Plantation Centre Food Court, opened its doors in May 2000, just nine months before Mac was born. It was the first Nu-Way to open in Macon in twenty-five years, since Northside broke ground in 1975.

There is More than One Way to Spell Wiener

Mac Garvin, who got a whiff of Nu-Way the day he was born, enjoys a Saturday tradition with his father, Ken, at Zebulon Road (Photo by Ed Grisamore)

The city's most famous hot dog found a hot spot in the northwest corner of the county, catching the front end of a major retail district. Soon Nu-Way was surrounded by a grocery store, movie theater, bank, school, church, apartment complexes, a retirement community, department stores, gas stations, a post office, motels and dozens of other restaurants.

"If we had not done this, I don't know where we would be today," said Dermatas.

The Zebulon Nu-Way sells hot dogs in one of the city's hot spots for local business development (Photo by Walter Elliott Photography)

STANTOM PLAZA

Bob Young was working as a curb boy at Fincher's Barbecue on Houston Avenue the day President Franklin D. Roosevelt died. He made a career working in the barbeque business, first at Fincher's, then running Young's Barbecue on Front Street from the early 1960s until 1974.

He now spends so much time at the Nu-Way in Stantom Plaza, he should probably have a stool named in his honor. He lives on Cherokee Drive, the street that runs behind the Nu-Way, just a half-mile from the front door. He can get there in one minute and forty-eight seconds if he slides through all the stop signs.

Bob arrives at Stantom Plaza every morning at 7 A.M. He is such a regular he usually gets the same parking place by the door.

"I can hear them playing reveille over at the base, and I know it's time to go over and get my coffee," he said.

He has been sitting on the same row of seats since 1974, often going with his wife, Gwin, who died in spring 2011.

The Nu-Way anchors the end of Stantom Plaza near Hickory Drive. Since it opened in 1969, it has been a gathering place for folks in the surrounding neighborhoods, many of them retired military or civil service workers from nearby Robins Air Force Base.

"A lot of them have been conditioned to be early risers, so they like a really good breakfast in the morning," said Cacavias. "They love the counter. You're in contact with everyone in that dining room. It's not like McDonald's when you get your food and go into a corner and have a private conversation."

Donna Savage, who is general manager of both Stantom Plaza and the newer store on Russell Parkway, said tradition should be an item on the menu as much as slaw dogs and chocolate malts.

"There's an older crowd that comes here," she said. "It's in the heart of this town, and everybody has eaten here for years. We cater to the older ones in these neighborhoods around here, and they love the counter."

Among the regulars is former Georgia governor Sonny Perdue, who has been dropping by for more than forty years.

Bob Young rises with reveille every morning to meet folks at the Nu-Way at Stantom Plaza, not far from his home in Warner Robins
(Photo by Ed Grisamore)

The Stantom Plaza Nu-Way is a traditional gathering spot for folks in Warner Robins (Photo courtesy of Nu-Way)

RUSSELL PARKWAY

Carson Hughes had never eaten at a Nu-Way until 2005, when he was seventeen years old. He went with some friends and wasn't quite sure what to order.

But there was one requirement.

Chili. Lots of chili.

So he ordered three hot dogs, chili only, and an order of chili fries.

"I was taking a gamble on it," he said. He knew nothing about Nu-Way's tradition and reputation for its fine chili sauce.

He now heads to the Nu-Way on Russell Parkway in Warner Robins at least once a week and orders the same meal every time. The Russell store is Nu-Way's newest, opening in 2000.

"I'm not even sure what else is on the menu," he said. "This is all I ever get."

The employees at the Russell restaurant may not always know him by name, but they know his face. And they know what he is going to order without him having to tell them. There are few surprises when he comes through the door after working all day as an F-15 mechanic at Robins Air Force Base.

"After a meal like that, it's time for a nap," he said, laughing.

FORT VALLEY

Jerry Scarborough has been going to the Nu-Way near Five Points in Fort Valley since it opened.

He was working nearby at Woolfolk Chemical, and there weren't many restaurant options in town at the time.

The Nu-Way has since moved a block down the street but Scarborough and his wife, Kay, are still among the loyal patrons. They usually show up for brunch. On Saturday mornings, it sometimes seems like half of Fort Valley is there, too.

Dermatas remembers when Nu-Way came to Peach County on the first day of May in 1972. It was the only time in the company's history when two stores opened the same month. (The Baconsfield location opened three weeks later.)

"I was a senior in high school, and I came down right after school that Friday," he said. "We didn't get out of there until 1 or 2 in the morning. I think it broke the

Carson Hughes has a date
with a chili dog at
Russell Parkway several
afternoons a week
(Photo by Ed Grisamore)

Jerry Scarborough, pictured with his wife, Kay, has been dining at the Nu-Way near Five Points in Fort Valley since it opened.
(Photo by Ed Grisamore)

all-time sales record. There wasn't a McDonald's or any other fast food in town, so they just came out of the woodwork. I've never see so many people in my life."

CHERRY STREET (R.I.P.)

It only lasted twenty years, but it was a good ride. The Nu-Way at 422 Cherry Street, the original Nu-Way No. 2, had to close in 1968 after a major fire in downtown Macon heavily damaged several businesses.

It was Cotton's first offspring, and fifteen more Nu-Ways would come after it over the next six decades.

Co-owner Gus Lolos kept the home grills burning on Cotton when George and Harry Andros left for World War II. When they returned after the war was over, there wasn't enough elbow room on Cotton for three owners, so the decision was made in 1948 to expand and open a second location.

They didn't have to go far. Only three-tenths of a mile separated the two restaurants.

Lolos managed the Cherry location and some of his faithful patrons followed him down the street. It was longer and wider than Cotton, with more seating. It was in a prime location for that part of downtown, especially since it was only a block from the Terminal Station, and Macon was a major rail transportation hub in the 1940s and '50s.

The fire broke out on January 23, 1968. The blaze began next door at a jewelry store and spread to Nu-Way. Both businesses sustained heavy losses and the buildings were gutted in the fire, which broke out in the early evening. Two firefighters were injured.

The Nu-Way on Cherry Street, as seen in 1948, the year it opened (Photo courtesy of Nu-Way)

Closing the Houston Avenue Nu-Way was a tough call in 2010 (Photo courtesy of Nu-Way)

HOUSTON AVENUE (R.I.P.)

It was the first suburban Nu-Way to open its doors. It boasted the first drive-thru window in Macon and one of the first in the state. Imagine that. You didn't even have to get out of your car to order a chili dog.

It was a big deal when it opened in June 1962, giving south Macon Nu-Wavians a place they could call their own.

For seven years, from 1962–1969, it was open on Sundays, too. It was a popular spot for the after-church crowd from nearby Mabel White Baptist. The Rev. Jimmy Waters even had his own special stool, right by the cash register.

The Nu-Way No. 3 catered heavily to the large companies and industries along Broadway, Houston Avenue, and Seventh Street. Large orders were often called in, and the employees would wrap the hot dogs in wax paper and place them in custom-made white boxes.

Florine Barrett was one of Houston Avenue's most unforgettable characters.

"She was just a simple country gal who walked in off the street one day, said she was hungry and needed a job, and my dad hired her," Cacavias said. "She had this wit about her. The customers loved her. Some of them called her Grandma, and she called them Grandpa. She had an incredible memory. She could remember six orders at a time without having to write anything down. Sometimes she would just tell people what they were going to have."

Closing the Houston Avenue Nu-Way on December 31, 2010, was an emotional day for Dermatas. It was where his father and John Cacavias had first started as managers. It was where he and Jim Cacavias had their first jobs as youngsters. It was his first managerial job after graduating from Georgia Tech in 1976.

It was heartbreaking to watch it decline.

"The economic development folks kept telling us the repaving of Houston Avenue was going to help the area, but we never saw it," he said. "Even after they finished with the road widening, our revenue kept going down for three straight years. It kept getting worse, so it was a bottom-line decision."

Former Macon fire chief B.H. Brown, a noted local artist, painted the famous Nu-Way boy and his dog, which became the Nu-Way logo
(Illustration courtesy of Nu-Way)

A Boy, His Dog, and the Chief

It started with a dog. A dog and a hot dog.

He was a saucy white-and-yellow Spitz who roamed the streets of Macon. He would show up along Cotton Avenue late every afternoon and beg for food on the sidewalk in front of Nu-Way.

No one knew his name or who owned him, just that he may have been the most well-fed dog this side of Rose Hill. And he knew how to work a crowd.

"He's the smartest beggar in town," owner George Andros told *The Macon Telegraph* in a story published on May 2, 1939.

Jimmy Hester, an attendant at the Nu-Way, started calling him "Sam," and the name stuck. He became known as "Sam the Beggar Dog."

Sam learned to pout, too. When things were too slow around the curbs, he would sometimes squeeze through the door at the Nu-Way. He had his own way of placing a to-go order.

"And I've just got to give him something," said Andros.

It would be another decade—about seventy-seven years in dog years—before a likeness of Sam would turn up as the inspiration behind the famous "boy and his dog" portrait that would become the Nu-Way logo and an icon in the hot dog world.

His name was Bernard Howard Brown, but he always went by his B. H. initials. He painted landscapes and biblical scenes for local churches. He did murals of the River Jordan for baptismal pools. He created backdrops for local stage productions at the Macon Little Theatre. He did work for several sign companies.

His specialties on canvas were paintings of snow scenes and bird dogs. They hung above mantels in homes from Shirley Hills to Cherokee Heights.

Chief B.H. Brown
(Courtesy of Macon-Bibb County Fire Department)

His day job was with the Macon Fire Department, where he worked for thirty-nine years. He started out as a plug man on the pump, rising through the ranks to driver, lieutenant, and captain. He served as fire chief from 1948 until his retirement in 1966. During his tenure as chief, the department added five new stations and doubled in size to 153 firemen. The fire department's headquarters on Oglethorpe Street was dedicated in his honor in 1975.

He was born in 1901 and never went to school past the second grade. He liked to draw as a youngster but didn't start taking it seriously until he was twenty-one. He began doing work for an advertising agency.

He had no formal art training. It started out as a hobby and evolved into working for local sign companies. For his own enjoyment, he would come home at night and paint at his family's home on Second Street. He had a studio in the basement when they moved to Woodhaven Road.

"He loved to paint, and he loved to give his paintings away," said his son, Curtis. "One of his paintings ended up all the way out in Walla Walla, Washington, and that person would send us a crate of apples every Christmas."

Curtis said a family friend, who ran a local printing operation, used to tease his father about all the snow scenes, telling him he was the only artist he knew who had to buy fifty-five-gallon drums of white paint.

"I remember him saying he was once offered a job painting sets for movies and stages, but he would have had to move to Texas and possibly California," said his youngest son, Ronald Brown. "My mother, Nell, didn't want to leave Macon, so he stayed here his whole life. He would claim he missed the money boat by not going with that stage group that wanted to hire him."

B. H. Brown always kept his easel at arm's reach, painting under the glow of a fluorescent light. In later years, he would prop a cue stick with a rubber ball attached at one end to steady his brush strokes.

One of his best-known works was a mural on the wall of the fire department's headquarters on First Street. It depicted a horse-drawn fire wagon he remembered from his childhood.

Ronald Brown said he still runs into folks who remember his father's paintings of bird dogs. But B. H. Brown's signature work of art was of another kind of a dog. A hot dog and a young boy.

It was like something right out of Norman Rockwell and the *Saturday Evening Post.*

The painting is of a boy, about nine or ten, with rolled-up pants and a slingshot in his pocket. He is clutching a newspaper under his left arm and looking over his right shoulder at a small black-and-white dog. The boy is holding a hot dog in his right hand, squeezing the bun so tightly mustard is squirting from the end.

Florrie Johnson said her father, Emory Clyde Matthews, always claimed that he was the young boy depicted in the painting. He and his six brothers grew up at the top of Cherry Street, near Magnolia, and he used to hawk copies of the newspaper on the street corners in downtown Macon. He later worked for the Macon Water Authority and died in 1974.

The painting never ended up in an art gallery. Instead, it became a gift to Nu-Way, where Brown was a regular. Ronald Brown remembers going to the Cotton Avenue Nu-Way lunch counter with his dad and seeing the print on the wall.

"I immediately recognized it as one of my dad's paintings," he said.

After one of the original paintings was stolen, it was replicated by local artists Ed Foster and Ann Rutland. Curtis Brown, who lives in Hawaii, has one of the originals in his home.

The image is now used as Nu-Way's official logo, printed on sacks, cups, hats, T-shirts, and fliers. On the Nu-Way website, it has been beamed all over the world.

It is the legacy of a talented and generous man.

Cathi Busbee, a Macon native now living in Metropolis, Illinois, makes the trip to Macon several times a year for her Nu-Way fix
(Photo by Ed Grisamore)

Going the Long Way

Cathi Schultz Busbee goes a long way for a Nu-Way.

She has no choice.

It is 478 miles from her home in Metropolis, Illinois, to the nearest Nu-Way in Macon, Georgia.

That's the round-trip equivalent of more than 10 million hot dogs lined up end to end to satisfy her craving for a Nu-Way. She takes the restaurant's famous slogan to heart.

Cathi lived in Macon in the 1960s and '70s. She and her family were regulars at the downtown Nu-Way on Cotton Avenue, and she remembers making frequent trips to Houston Avenue, Bloomfield, and Napier Square.

"I grew up on Nu-Ways and a chocolate malt," she said. "It was always a real treat. We never lived very far away from a Nu-Way."

A few years after she graduated from Southwest High School in 1974, she worked at the Piggly Wiggly grocery store on Northside Drive. She would make regular trips across the parking lot to the Nu-Way.

Her husband, Allen, was a Bibb County deputy sheriff who was raised on them, too. When he retired in 2003, they moved to Illinois.

It didn't take long before the Nu-Way withdrawals began.

"I tried to make them, but there was no way I could duplicate them," she said. "A plain hot dog and a can of chili just doesn't work. And the rest of the food selection in Yankee Land was not so good. You can't get things like butterbeans and country fried steak."

So, one night she turned to Allen and told him if she didn't have a chili dog in a steamed bun real soon she was going to be pushed right over the edge.

"I'm thinking about making a food run to Georgia," she said.

She waited until the snow thawed in the spring and began planning her trip. It proved to be costly from the very beginning. The Busbees only had one car, so she had to rent a Nissan Altima for the trip south down I-24 and I-75.

Cathi left on a Friday with a sense of urgency, knowing Nu-Way is closed on Sundays. She carried two large ice chests and pulled into the parking lot in Baconsfield at 11 A.M. on Saturday and walked up to the counter.

She ordered 150 "all the way" to go and watched their jaws drop.

"They called the manager and told me I might have to wait for a little while," she said. "I told them it was no problem. They were all so nice. They had never had someone come off the street like that and order so many hot dogs at one time. I told them I was from Illinois and showed them my driver's license."

She was amused when one of the employees asked her: "Do you want fries with that?"

She asked them to put two hot dogs to the side, and she ate them while she waited.

They double-wrapped each hot dog, and she took them to her daughter's home in Gray. They stuck them in the freezer overnight. The next morning, they placed the frozen hot dogs in large Ziploc bags, then put them in the coolers on ice.

"I got them back to Illinois, and it was a taste of home," Cathi said. "It was gold."

Whenever she and Allen got a hankering for a home dog, Cathi would thaw them, take the hot dog out of the bun and heat it separately in the microwave for forty-five seconds. Then she would place both the hot dog and the bun in the microwave for another fifteen seconds.

Cathi said they loved to share the Nu-Ways with some of their Illinois neighbors, but Allen was never generous with their supply.

"He was very particular who he gave them to," she said. "And nobody ever got more than one."

Over the years, Cathi has made it a tradition to schedule three or four Nu-Way trips a year. Allen died in October 2009, but she still makes the journey in his memory. She just doesn't order as many hot dogs to go.

"I keep the number for the Baconsfield Nu-Way in my cell phone directory," she said, laughing. "Now, I always call them when I'm on my way. I tell them it's the crazy lady from Illinois."

The News Way

The late Lewis Grizzard was a man who knew how to use a fork.

He wrote about barbecue, butterbeans, creamed potatoes, sliced tomatoes. and country fried steak smothered with sawmill gravy. He was convinced instant grits were some kind of communist plot, and he never met a piece of fried chicken he didn't like. He believed if you ate something, but nobody saw you eat it, then it had no calories.

The Atlanta newspaper columnist's down-home humor drew comparisons to a modern-day Mark Twain. He published more than two dozen books, including *Chili Dawgs Always Bark at Night*, in December 1990. On the cover, Grizzard is surrounded by hot dogs. Inside, he wrote about what he called his "dogged addiction to chili dogs."

"Those wonderful hot dogs with lots of chili on them and mustard and onions on the chili that the mere mention of which makes my mouth water, my heart rate speed up, and my stomach literally beg to be fed as many of these delights as it can possibly hold," he wrote.

Grizzard had a penchant for putting a good eating place on the map. If he espoused the virtues of the cheeseburgers at some Atlanta-area truck stop or raved about the hoecakes at a hole-in-the-wall in south Georgia, it was instant credibility in the minds of his loyal readers.

When Grizzard stopped at the Blue Willow in Social Circle in March 1992, his glowing review helped the struggling restaurant turn the corner. Soon, the phone was ringing and the calls were coming in from all over the country. The restaurant later enclosed the porch for additional seating, and it was named in Grizzard's honor.

He was especially fond of Sprayberry's in Newnan, not far from his hometown of Moreland. The restaurant's owners named his favorite barbecue plate the "Lewis Grizzard Special" following his death in 1994.

So when Grizzard sang the praises of Nu-Way in a column in February 1986, it was worth its weight in golden mustard.

He listed what he called "the Nu-Way Weinie joint in Macon" as one of the world's outstanding restaurants.

As flattering as it was to be mentioned by one of the country's best-known newspaper columnists, it was a two-minute spot in an hour-long documentary on public television in June 1999 that took Nu-Way to a new level of name recognition.

When narrator Rick Sebak visited the twenty-two best hot dog restaurants in America, Nu-Way was on his short list. He called hot dogs "maybe as close as we'll ever get to a national dish."

A Hot Dog Program was promoted by PBS as "an all-American celebration of those fabulous and phenomenally popular little sausages in those soft little buns" and an "entertaining look at what may be the country's most popular food."

Noting that the Macon weiner institution had been around longer than any hot dog establishment except for Nathan's in New York, Sebak told viewers, "It's called Nu-Way, but it's really old."

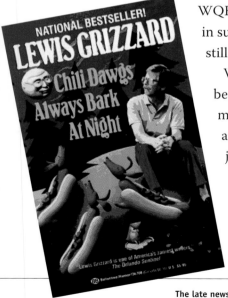

Sebak, an award-winning television producer with WQED in Pittsburgh, arrived with his film crew in Macon in summer 1998. The documentary aired a year later and is still being repeated on PBS more than ten years later.

When the PBS documentary aired in June, it proved to be a banner month on Cotton Avenue. Nu-Way also was mentioned in the *Smithsonian* magazine in a feature article titled "Hot Dogs Are Us." And a couple of radio disc jockeys in Arizona conducted an online survey to find the most popular hot dog hangouts. Underdog Nu-Way won the contest, beating out some of the more famous hot dog havens in New York, Chicago, and Pittsburgh.

After that, the hits just kept on coming.

The late newspaper columnist Lewis Grizzard once lauded Nu-Way as one of the world's outstanding restaurants (Book cover courtesy of Ballantine Books)

"A Hot Dog Program" began airing on PBS in 1999 and featured Nu-Way as one of the 22 best hot dog restaurants in the land
(Photo courtesy of PBS)

In its January 2000 issue, *Money* magazine tapped Nu-Way as "the definitive downtown hot-dog lunch venue." The Varsity in Atlanta made the same list of nine restaurants, but granddaddy Nathan's in New York did not.

The magazine also sang the praises of the "magnificent vintage neon sign" along with "friendly waitresses, cozy booths, and a sociable crowd."

Southern Living gave Nu-Way a shout-out in its August 2001 issue, when staff writer Cassandra Vanhooser wrote a two-page article, confessing to have become a fan after sitting down with one of the restaurant's hot dogs—all the way, of course.

"I used to scoff at the Nu-Way Weiners slogan, but all that changed the day I tasted one of their famous chili dogs," she wrote. "Now, just mention Macon, Georgia, and my mouth starts to water."

She quoted Dermatas as he described the "craving" of Nu-Way aficionados and compared the insatiable taste as "almost like an addiction."

She was sold.

"I think it's only fair to warn you: Once you sink your teeth into a Nu-Way, there's no turning back," she wrote.

Gourmet magazine proclaimed Nu-Way as "one of America's ten best hot dog joints" in its October 2001 issue. The magazine's "Roadfood" columnists, Michael and Jane Stern, described Nu-Way as "a shoebox-shaped restaurant with instantaneous service and addictive hot dogs."

Nu-Way was one of only two hot dog restaurants in the South to make the cut. Skin Thrasher's in Anderson, South Carolina, which opened in 1946 in a former pool hall, was the other. (It was named after founder Lloyd T. Thrasher, whose friends started calling him "Skin" after he got a short haircut.)

The Roadfood authors were impressed with Nu-Way's "vivid red links grilled and bedded in soft buns and are best topped with mustard, onions and a fine-grained chili with a barbecue sauce zing. To go whole hog, creamy-sweet coleslaw can be ladled to complete the package."

In July 2002, the *New York Times* Sunday food section would laud Nu-Way's slaw dogs as "the acknowledged king of this particular hill," introducing the local legend to a nation of hot dog lovers.

In August 2003, viewers of NBC's *Today* show got a taste of Nu-Way on the air. A crew from the show stopped by the Macon landmark while shooting a summer travel piece on Macon, Atlanta, and Savannah. It featured a quartet of young men—Trey "Eddie" Gibbons, Victor "Vincent" Lyons, Xavier "Frank" Davis, and Sharone "Rocko" Davis—known as "The Nu-Way Doo-Wops." They sang the same jingle now featured on Nu-Way's website (www.nu-wayweiners.com)

The Travel Channel traveled "a long way for a Nu-Way" in June 2004.

The slaw dog took another bow in the April 2007 issue of *Every Day With Rachel Ray.* The feature was called "Dogville: When you're ordering a hot dog, location is everything." The grilled slaw dog was pictured in a lineup with hot dogs from New York City, Chicago, Los Angeles, and New Jersey.

If capturing the attention of magazines and newspapers in the print media wasn't exciting enough, the words soon began appearing more permanently in books.

Leading the way was John T. Edge, who grew up in nearby Jones County and serves as director of the Southern Foodways Alliance at the Center for the Study of Southern Culture at Ole Miss.

Edge paid homage to Nu-Way as a culinary icon in his 2007 book, *Southern Belly: The Ultimate Food Lover's Companion to the South.*

"Before The Varsity was even a twinkle in founder Frank Gordy's eye, Nu-Way Weiners was doing a booming business," wrote Edge, the author of nine other books on the culture of food. "Famous since 1916 for the sweet heat of the chili sauce on the dogs, the flaky ice in the cups of Coke, and the dark, rich chocolate milk, served icy-cold to generations of Macon children, this local chain may well have been the model for its more famous rival in Atlanta."

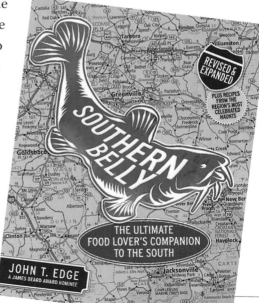

Author Becky Mercuri made reference to Nu-Way's slaw dogs in *The Great American Hot Dog Book.* David Graulich included Nu-Way in the "Local Legends" section of his book, *The Hot Dog Companion: All About the Foods We Love to Eat—With a Side of Guilt.*

John T. Edge's Southern Belly gave a shout-out to Nu-Way along the way
(Photo courtesy of Algonquin Books)

Locally, *Macon Magazine* writers James and Jodi Palmer and Paige Henson took note of Nu-Way's amazing run of national publicity and bestowed an honor itself. In the magazine's winter 2007 issue, it awarded Nu-Way a "Perfect 10" in a list of "tried and true parts of Macon that are always worth celebrating."

"Not only is it a long-standing great thing about Macon," said the article, "but it's gaining 'great thing' status in the world of hot dogs."

Co-owner Spyros Dermatas said he has been humbled and honored by all the media attention Nu-Way has received in recent years.

"My first thought is about all of the fiercely loyal customers we have been so lucky to have had for so many decades because without them, we would not be here today," he said. "I thank all of them from the bottom of my heart! And I think about my father, Nick Dermatas, and my godfather, Gus Lolos, and all the other owners, managers, and employees who preceded us, and worked so hard to make all of this possible. I wish my father could have been here to experience all of this. He loved Nu-Way so much."

Ruth Sykes, of the Macon-Bibb County Convention and Visitors Bureau, grew up eating Nu-Way hot dogs. And it didn't take much to convert her Savannah-native husband, John.

She even gave him a cross-stitch of the *Boy and Dog* for an engagement present. She still laughs about the time he showed up at a wedding after stopping at Nu-Way on the way over.

"He brought tears to everybody's eyes, not because of the wedding but because of all those onions he ate," she said.

She has seen it have the same effect on tourists.

"They come by and want to know how to get to Nu-Way," she said. "A lot of times they will have read about it in *Southern Living* or from a travel writer for a newspaper. They will bring the articles with them. We send them up there, and sometimes they come back to tell us how good it was. I love having the bragging rights to a place with such notoriety."

And the Weiner Is...

When Cathy Riley was pregnant with her son, Rob, she ate at Nu-Way almost every day. She had cravings for them morning, noon, and night.

After the stork arrived five weeks early, her mom used to tease her it was because all those chili dogs were restless.

Rob grew up to love Nu-Way hot dogs almost as much as his mother. And so did his baby sister, Lucy.

Cathy took them to Nu-Way every Saturday. It became a family tradition. "That's how they knew it was Saturday," she said, laughing.

So it didn't really surprise her when Lucy came home in the fifth grade at Winship Magnet School in 1999 and announced she was going to do her social science project on Nu-Way.

"We were told we could pick anything for our project, and I wanted to do something unique," said Lucy, now twenty-three. "My teacher said I could do it on food, and I thought of Nu-Way. It had a history to it."

Cathy, who was a paraprofessional at the school, was pretty excited about it. It would be fun helping her daughter with some of the research.

Not to mention delicious.

She called co-owner Jim Cacavias and asked if it would be OK if she brought Lucy to the Nu-Way office to interview them and take some pictures. Sure, Jim said. It was not unusual for the Nu-Way owners to get requests from young people doing research for class projects or term papers. They would usually invite them to come by the corporate office on Cotton Avenue, where the walls are lined with fascinating memorabilia and the restaurant's rich history neatly archived in three-ring binders.

Lucy's presentation included an actual hot dog bun mounted on the display. Little did she know she was going to have to keep replacing the bread each time.

Why? Because she kept winning. And winning. And winning.

The winning part never got stale.

After taking first place in her school competition, she advanced to the area competition where she received another blue ribbon. Then came regionals at Macon State College, and she was back in the winner's circle again.

The principal would announce each victory over the intercom, and pretty soon the whole school rallied behind her as she proudly carried the Winship banner.

The state contest was also held at Macon State College. Lucy won't ever forget the date. It was her eleventh birthday—March 17, 1999. And she had never had such a full plate in her life.

The day began at Freedom Park, where she had a softball game and her team photograph was made for Picture Day. Then, she headed to Macon State with her mom for the contest judging. She had another softball game that afternoon.

"I hit a home run," she said.

Lucy Riley, with co-owner Jim Cacavias in 1999. Lucy was a fifth-grader at Winship Elementary when her school project on Nu-Way won a national contest and she was interviewed by The History Channel (Photo courtesy of Nu-Way)

It was nothing compared to the grand slam she hit when they announced the results of the judging. Wearing a Nu-Way cap and shirt, she had won the state competition, qualifying her project for the national contest in New York.

"Spyros and Jim followed us all the way," said Cathy. "They gave her class a big party at the end of the year, catered by Nu-Way. We had hot dogs, hamburgers, and tea with flaky ice. Spyros did a trivia contest and everyone in the class got either a hat or a T-shirt."

After it was announced Lucy had won the national competition, a film crew from The History Channel came to interview her about the project. She also received a $200 savings bond. Nu-Way contributed a $100 savings bond.

She found herself speaking to the Middle Georgia Historical Society at the Sidney Lanier Cottage. Her project was put on display at the Georgia Music Hall of Fame.

Lucy still thinks about those wonderful days at Winship. The experience helped shape her.

"It was such a big part of my life," she said. "It gave me such self-confidence. Not every eleven-year-old gets to do the kinds of things I got to do. I had support from my family, my school, the community, and from people who didn't even know me. They showed a lot of love to a little kid."

Even now, when she gets a whiff of a chili dog or feels the cold crunch of flaky ice or drives past the sign with the misspelled hot dog, it will take her down memory lane.

"Whenever somebody mentions Nu-Way, I will say, 'Well, when I was in the fifth grade....'"

(Above) Lucy Riley, now attending college, still loves talking about her famous history project (Photo courtesy of the Riley Family)

TV talk show hostess Oprah Winfrey stopped at Nu-Way in November 2007 while filming two shows in Macon. "The cult following was unbelievable," said co-owner Spyros Dermatas (Photo courtesy of Steve Wilson)

The Oprah Effect

Whenever and wherever she moved, the crowds moved with her.

From College Street to Cotton Avenue, they staked spots along her path to catch a glimpse. Or maybe get an autograph or snap a photograph. Would she come this way? Or would she go that way?

From the first day the goddess showed up, there were Oprah sightings all over town.

Her legions of loyal fans camped out on the lawn of the 1842 Inn, the bed and breakfast where she rested her head on fluffy pillows every night.

They wanted to know where she was going to eat and where she was going to shop. It was as if Macon had its own paparazzi.

It was an amazing time in an amazing place.

In 2007, producers for television host Oprah Winfrey determined an average of 45 percent of television sets in Macon tuned into her show every afternoon at 4 P.M., more than any city in the country per capita.

The *Oprah Winfrey Show*, which began broadcasting nationally in September 1986, eventually became the highest-rated program of its kind in television history.

She had her highest ratings ever in 2007, which influenced her decision to bring her production crew to the city that provided her most prolific fan base. Oprah announced she would tape two shows in Macon in November.

A local newspaper columnist wrote a front-page story the day she arrived, suggesting some of the things she could see, do, and eat during her visit. There was considerable speculation she might head over to the Nu-Way for a slaw dog. After all, it was only a half-block away from the Macon City Auditorium, where she would be taping her show.

Nu-Way employee Jasmine Henderson was convinced Oprah would be walking through those doors at lunchtime on the Friday afternoon of November 9. In fact, she asked her mother, manager Veronica Smith, to put her on that shift.

A few days earlier, a Macon television crew showed up at the Nu-Way to interview employees about the possibility Oprah would be dining on Cotton Avenue.

"When everybody else ran away from the camera, I stepped up and said I felt like she was going to come because that's what people do when they come to Macon," Jackson said. "They go to Nu-Way."

Co-owners Spyros Dermatas and Jim Cacavias knew there was a chance the world's most famous television personality might be popping in for a visit. They wanted to be prepared but, at the same time, try not to get their hopes too high. After all, chili-dogs and Mega-Burgers might not be on Oprah's much-publicized diet.

"The word on the street that morning was she was going to H&H to eat with Mama Louise," said Dermatas. "Two hours before lunch, someone told us the entourage was headed to H&H, so we really didn't think she was coming."

H&H is also a Macon dining institution, located three-tenths of a mile up the hill on Forsyth Street and known for its soul food. It gained fame in the 1970s when the Allman Brothers and other Southern rock bands would wander a block up Cotton Avenue from Capricorn Recording Studio to Five Points.

Co-owner Louise Hudson would serve them fried chicken, pork chops, okra, collard greens, macaroni and cheese (considered a vegetable in the South), and iced tea in mason jars.

Jasmine was almost in denial.

"I had gotten my hopes up, so I was upset when everyone started talking about her going to the H&H instead," she said. "Some of them told me, 'Oh, she doesn't want one of those hot dogs!'"

When Oprah arrived at H&H, she was surrounded by security guards. She entered the restaurant through the back door to the kitchen. She signed autographs for fans but did not sit down to eat.

Dermatas looked up and down the sidewalk on Cotton Avenue. The crowds stretched over to Cherry Street and up Cotton toward City Hall. He walked over to the SunTrust Bank at the corner of Cherry and Second Street.

Oprah's effect on Nu-Way? "Suddenly people all over the world were calling us asking if they could order hot dogs," said co-owner Jim Cacavias

(Photo courtesy of Steve Wilson)

"People were just milling about and waiting," he said. "The cult following was unbelievable."

And then he saw her, with three SUVs and five film crews in tow. She had gone into a shoe boutique on Cherry Street owned by Karla Redding Andrews, daughter of famed soul singer Otis Redding.

Cacavias went to his car parked near the loading dock in the back and left to make the rounds at some of the other Nu-Way restaurants in town. He pulled down an alley toward Cherry Street and watched a huge crowd following Oprah. He, too, noticed all the commotion.

"It was crazy," he said. "She was like a magnet. The more she walked on the street, the more people started gathering and following."

By then, all eyes were on the "Best Weiner in Town" neon sign. Would that be the Pavlov's hot dog for the Oprah crew?

"I came in through the kitchen door and told Veronica to be expecting her," said Dermatas. "I thought Veronica and Jasmine were going to start hyperventilating. I told them they could take care of it by themselves, and I would be in the back if they needed me. I wanted it to be their moment. I wanted them to be able to revel in the excitement."

One customer who was eating in the restaurant told Veronica to hurry up and serve him. He knew everybody would stop in their tracks when Oprah walked through the door.

About that time, Oprah and her bodyguards came in.

"Spyros (Dermatas) had told me to introduce myself and tell her about four generations of my family working at the Nu-Way," said Veronica. "But I forgot everything. I just went right off and left the register. I don't even know who was taking the money after that."

Years earlier, Veronica had been working behind the counter when another celebrity came by the restaurant. Howard E. Rollins, an actor who played the role of Virgil Tibbs on the television show *In the Heat of the Night*, stopped by to eat in the heat of the day. She got his autograph on a Nu-Way plate. (Rollins had played the role of Andrew Young in *King* about Martin Luther King Jr. Some of the movie's scenes were filmed in Macon. He was later nominated for an Academy Award for best supporting actor in the 1981 movie *Ragtime*.)

But this was different. It was like she was in a dream. She looked over at her daughter. Jasmine was standing by the microwave. She was crying.

Oprah saw Jasmine and walked over to her.

"Oh my, why are you crying?" she asked her.

Jasmine reached for words that did not come.

"My heart was beating so fast," she said. "I couldn't believe I was standing next to Oprah Winfrey. I was speechless."

Veronica grabbed her camera and began taking pictures.

Duncan Matthews, who works with the investigative drug unit for the Bibb County Sheriff's Department, admitted he may have been the only soul in Macon who had not known Oprah was in town.

He was sitting alone in his usual booth, second from the door, nibbling on his Mega-Burger when all heck broke loose.

"This big guy came up and told me I was going to have to move," he said. "He said this was Oprah's booth. And I told him I didn't think so. It was Duncan's booth. And then there was Oprah, and she asked if she could sit down with me."

She was very nice. She asked him questions about his job and family. He teased her about her order. "If you order two chili dogs and fries, then what's the point of getting a Diet Coke?" he told her.

For the record, she ordered two hot dogs "all the way" with fries and a medium Diet Coke. (She later ordered a third hot dog but only ate half of it.)

Duncan called his wife, Sheila, who thought he was playing a joke on her. But Oprah talked to her on Duncan's cell phone for a few minutes.

"Then I told her I was probably the only man in America who would break his date with Oprah," said Duncan. "But I had to go serve a search warrant."

Dermatas could hear the excitement from his office next door. The Oprahfication of Nu-Way was resounding through the walls. After she finished eating, he walked into the restaurant and introduced himself.

"She was so polite and down to earth," he said. "I thanked her for coming. She told me the hot dogs were fabulous."

Local attorney Steve Wilson, a regular at the Nu-Way, walked through a back alley from Cherry Street and went in through the kitchen to get a peek at the television celebrity in the crowded restaurant.

"The real show at the Nu-Way was not Oprah," he said. "The show was the people watching Oprah."

For days, weeks and months, the Oprah effect lingered. The neon sign out front was practically glowing on its own.

Oprah taped her "My Favorite Things" show the next day at the City Auditorium. A second show from Macon aired a week later, documenting her stay in Macon and trips to restaurants, shops, museums, and homes.

When asked about some of her own "favorite things" about her visit, she mentioned the "hot dogs from the Nu-Way."

"It's hard to believe one person could come for a visit and the whole nation was watching," said Cacavias. "Suddenly, people from all over the world were calling us asking if they could order hot dogs. We sent frozen hot dogs all over. Sales of our T-shirts spiked."

Oprah's culinary cascade through Macon did not go unnoticed by the gossip tabloids. A month later, the *National Enquirer* hit the news stands with a two-page "story" titled "Oprah Eats Her Way through Macon, Ga."

The magazine claimed Oprah consumed 10,700 calories in 48 hours and that her weight had become "so out of control that she's risking her health and turning herself into a ticking time bomb." The story alleged she ate 532 grams of fat, including 166 grams of saturated fat.

In reference to her trip to the Nu-Way, the magazine fed this sentence to "Enquiring" minds: "Oprah scarfed down three hot dogs piled high with coleslaw and other fixings, a large order of fries and a thirty-two-ounce soft drink."

Jim later said he never used the words "scarfed" or "piled with coleslaw and other fixings" when the *Enquirer* reporter contacted him. He called the story "garbage."

Jasmine still keeps a photo of herself and Oprah posted on her Facebook page. She has something to share with her children, and one day, her grandchildren.

"Every time I saw her on TV after that I wanted to write her show to see if she remembered me," said Jasmine. "I wanted to ask her if she remembered the girl from the hot dog place who was crying."

Family Matters

Johnny Nicholas was born in Macon in 1920, just four years after James Mallis opened the city's first fast-food restaurant on Cotton Avenue.

His parents, Pete and Cynthia Nicholas, were among the first Greek families to settle in Macon. George and Harry Andros, who later became owners of the restaurant, once lived with Johnny and his family. As a child, his father would take him for lunch at the Nu-Way every Sunday after services at Christ Church.

"I would get a hot dog and chocolate milk," he said. "Hot dogs cost a nickel back then."

Johnny started working at the Mulberry Market when he was sixteen. Then, after World War II, he returned as a meat cutter and began dating a pretty cashier named Fay. It was love at first slice, and they married.

One of Johnny's first accounts at Mulberry was to supply the ground beef for Nu-Way's hamburgers. The Mulberry Market eventually became known as Mulberry Provision. He stayed there until 1969, when he left to become manager at the Nu-Way at Napier Square.

Fay worked both in Nu-Way's front office and spent time at the restaurants in Baconsfield, Northside, Houston Avenue and Bloomfield. A photograph of her hangs on the wall in the Cotton Avenue location.

The couple's two daughters, Beverly and Gail, both worked for them. Nu-Way's current owners—cousins Spyros Dermatas and Jim Cacavias— trained under them when they were teenagers.

When Beverly was named manager at the city's newest Nu-Way on Zebulon Road, she asked her parents to help out part-time at the store.

They agreed…under one condition.

"When we're working, I told her to treat us just like any other employees," said Johnny. "When we leave, we can be her mom and dad again."

Their official title? Goodwill ambassadors. They knew almost everybody who came through the door at the Plantation Centre Food Court.

Five days a week, you could find Johnny in the kitchen grilling hot dogs while Fay would work the front counter and dining room. They would ride together to work every day except Tuesday, when Miss Fay left early to get her hair done.

"We are not rocking chair people," Johnny once said. "We've got to get out. We are 'people' people. The Lord has blessed us with good health. This is something to get up for every morning. We see old friends here and make new ones."

They both retired in 2011, Johnny at the age of ninety-one and Fay at eighty-seven.

. . .

Veronica Smith's family tree runs from Cotton Avenue to Emery Highway to Cherry Street to Houston Avenue.

(Left) Johnny Nicholas retired from Nu-Way in 2011, at the age of 91 (Photo courtesy of Woody Marshall, The Macon Telegraph)
(Center) Fay Nicholas worked at the drive-thru window at Napier Square in the 1970s (Photo courtesy of Nu-Way)

It spans sixty years of steamed buns and four generations of spooning chili to loyal customers so punctual you could set your watch by them.

Veronica is manager of Nu-Way No. 1, the flagship restaurant downtown on Cotton Avenue. She has been working at Nu-Way for twenty-four years, following in the footsteps of her mother, Ethel Hawkins, and grandmother, the late Mary Smith. Veronica's daughter, Jasmine Henderson, and son, Quinn Hollis, are fourth-generation Nu-Way employees.

Mary Smith started working at the Nu-Way in the 1940s, and her paychecks stretched across the 1950s and '60s. She was a single mother raising nine children. Ethel was third from the oldest.

"She was sweet, kind and hard-working," said Ethel. "If you did something wrong, she would get you. She kept all of us children in line. The rules of the house were you had to work hard and be obedient. She was very spiritual. We would come home from church, clean up, and she would always cook a big meal on Sunday."

At work one day, co-owner John Cacavias walked in the kitchen. Mary was peeling onions.

"You know, Mary, you're very efficient," he said.

(Right) Cotton Avenue manager Veronica Smith, center, with her mother, Ethel Hawkins, daughter Jasmine Henderson and son Quinn Hollis (Photo by Ed Grisamore)

She was so offended she stormed out the back door. She wasn't sure what "efficient" meant, but she sure didn't think he was paying her a compliment.

It took a while, but John got it straightened out and smoothed over.

Harry Andros once held up Mary as a model to the other employees, telling them one Mary could outwork five of them.

Ethel and two of her sisters and a brother also held jobs at Nu-Way. Ethel began working when she was eleven years old. She started at Cherry Street until a fire closed the restaurant, then transferred to Houston Avenue, and later to Baconsfield when it opened. She put in more than thirty years with the company.

"I did just about everything, but I loved to cook," Ethel said. "The more I worked, the better I felt. I could load the hot dogs up my arm and work fast."

She was at the Houston Avenue restaurant when current co-owners Jim Cacavias and Spyros Dermatas began working there as youngsters. Jim's father, John Cacavias, would give her a ride home after work. Spyros's father, Nick Dermatas, would pay for her to go to the movies at the Douglass Theatre when she worked on Cherry Street.

"I would be watching the movie, but if they got real busy over on Cherry they would call me back in," she said. "They would call my name on the intercom, right in the middle of the movie."

Veronica started at the Baconsfield Nu-Way as a teenager. Her family was living in a housing project called Felton Homes, sometimes known as "Alphabet City" because the streets are named after letters in the alphabet.

"We had what we needed, but we lacked some things," she said. "We used to wear passed-down clothes. I remember my first paycheck was for $18, and I thought it was a million dollars."

She paid her dues, working the circuit from Baconsfield to Bloomfield to Northside Drive. She was named manager in 1997, left for a few years, then returned in 2000 and has been there ever since.

A former employee, Brenda Riley, started calling Veronica "Boss Lady," and the name stuck.

"She used to pick at me because I thought I was an authority on everything," Veronica said, laughing. "Now everybody calls me 'Boss Lady.'"

She said she appreciates what Nu-Way has done for her and her family.

"They love loyalty," she said. "And, when you are loyal, they make you feel like part of the family."

• • •

Diana Bailey knows about family.

In thirty-three years working at Nu-Way, she has had hundreds of brothers, sisters, sons, daughters, nieces, nephews, and cousins.

They all wear red shirts with a yellow Nu-Way emblem right next to their hearts.

Diana never married, so she claims her co-workers as kinfolks.

"She is like a sister to us," said Dermatas.

The feeling is mutual, although Diana loves to tease him and blame him that he's the reason she's never worn a wedding ring on her left hand.

"I tell him I never got married because they worked me to death," she said, laughing. "And that I got fat because they didn't pay me enough so I had to eat Nu-Way all the time. And that my hands do all this work, so nobody is going to want to hold my hand."

She first started working under Beverly Nicholas at Napier, which was near her home in Bellevue. She left to go back to school and was working at the Medical Center when Beverly called and asked if she could fill in some at Napier at breakfast until she could hire somebody full-time.

Diana said yes. That "temporary" job has lasted more than thirty years.

She started at Northside just a few months after it opened in 1975 and has been there ever since. She has seen more than a generation of customers come through the restaurant.

"I have people come in all the time and ask me if I remember them," she said. "They want to know if I remember they used to ride their bike down here or they worked at the Piggly Wiggly."

Diana Bailey runs a tight ship at Northside and has trained a number of Nu-Way managers (Photo by Ed Grisamore)

Some claim she makes the best hot dogs in the chain. "You have to have a special touch," she said. "They have to be hot and right off the grill. I don't like it when you have to move them to the side. They should have that sizzle."

She has trained almost half of Nu-Way's current managers. In 2011, she became general manager of both Northside and Zebulon after Beverly Nicholas had to take medical leave.

"We have been so fortunate to have this lady," Dermatas said. "She is such a good family person. I can't say enough about her."

◆ ◆ ◆

It gets hot in the kitchen, but Johnnie Mae Parker never seems to mind.

The grill can be bringing home the bacon, the oil can be turning those fries golden brown, and the steam can be rising from the bun machine, but you won't find her complaining.

She grew up picking cotton in the fields of Twiggs County, so this is a piece of cake. Or, since she works at Nu-Way, make that a hot apple turnover.

"I've been out there hoeing in the fields when it was cold and hot, and you could look up and see snakes in the trees," she said. "So I told myself if I ever got a job where I could work inside, I'm staying."

She worked off and on at Nu-Way for a few years, then came back for good in April 1986. She cooks everything in the kitchen at Baconsfield, which is the No. 1 restaurant in the company in terms of volume.

Johnnie Mae Parker is a staple in the kitchen at Baconsfield, the top volume restaurant in the Nu-Way chain (Photo by Ed Grisamore)

Johnnie Mae rarely gets flustered when the line is backed up to the door and there are eight cars in the drive-thru.

She's sixty-eight years old going on sixteen. She can handle every grilled ham and cheese and sausage and egg biscuit order that comes down the line.

"She doesn't like for anybody to help her," said manager Diana Hunter. "And she moves so fast my daughter [Gail] calls her 'The Tornado.'"

. . .

For more than thirty years, Barbara Johnson has fed the multitudes.

She has satisfied the appetites for the lunch crowd at Bloomfield and helped break the fasts of both the early risers and brunch bunch at Napier Square.

"I'm ready to go and start putting things on the grill every morning at 6:30," she said.

She loves her job almost as much as she loves the chili dogs. It's a fringe benefit of working at the Nu-Way.

"We have people at Napier who eat breakfast every morning," she said. "They sit around and swap stories. Some of them come back for lunch. Some of them even come back for supper."

. . .

Ray Mills lived in the margins of life.

Anyone who followed him kept an eraser at the end of their pencils. He lived under so many different roofs he would often head home trying to remember which key fit the lock.

The one place that was always home, though, was the Nu-Way on Cotton

Barbara Johnson keeps things straight in the kitchen at Napier Square (Photo by Ed Grisamore)

Avenue. For thirty-two years, Ray clocked in six days a week and saved his odd jobs for Sunday.

Oh, there were pockets of interruptions. He spent some time in jail. His personnel file was as thick as his fist.

But owners Cacavias and Dermatas helped him clear his name, pay his bills, and knock back the demons. After all, Ray could handle the workload of three employees. And nobody took greater pride in their work.

He made the chili and slaw for all the Nu-Way restaurants. He cooked nearly a half-ton of chili every week. He diced some 300,000 pounds of cabbage in his lifetime.

Yes, he fought the slaw. And the slaw won.

Ronnie Marshall worked side-by-side with Ray for more than twenty years. They shed a lot of tears together, mostly when they chopped onions. Ronnie would chew on a wooden matchstick to ward off the watery eyes. But Ray would always tough it out.

There were plenty of tears—hold the onions—in April 2009 when Ray's three-pack-a-day cigarette habit caught up with him, and the lung cancer ended his life at age fifty-eight.

He had blue-collar roots in south Macon. He once worked for the circus, putting up tents and rides. Then he and his wife dined at the Nu-Way one spring evening in 1977, and his life changed forever.

Dermatas can still remember where Ray sat (third booth from the door) and what he ordered (two burgers all the way with hot sauce).

More importantly, he remembers it was the night Ray asked him for a job.

"He was like a jack rabbit, energetic and full of life," Dermatas said. "He was always eager to please."

The late Ray Mills once made the chili and slaw for all Nu-Way restaurants (Photo courtesy of Nu-Way)

"There were no limits to his work ethic," Cacavias said. "He would get things so clean he would almost wipe the paint off the finish."

Ray didn't own a car. He either caught the bus or walked. He knew every shortcut and every downtown alley. He was scrawny but strong, and he always tried to appear tougher than he was. He would sometimes arrive at work with tall tales of switchblade-wielding attackers.

He never traveled far. If he ever told you he went to the beach, he usually meant Lake Tobesofkee.

He always looked forward to going to Atlanta for the annual Taste of Macon during the state General Assembly, too. Whenever someone would rave about the chili or slaw, he would raise his hand, thump his chest, and proudly boast that he made it.

Ray couldn't read, so it never really mattered that Nu-Way's neon sign has intentionally misspelled "weiners" since 1937.

He didn't have any teeth, either, but the man could chew up an apple and gnaw down a piece of fried chicken.

Despite his flaws and imperfections, he was genuine.

"He was a character," Cacavias said. "One of a kind."

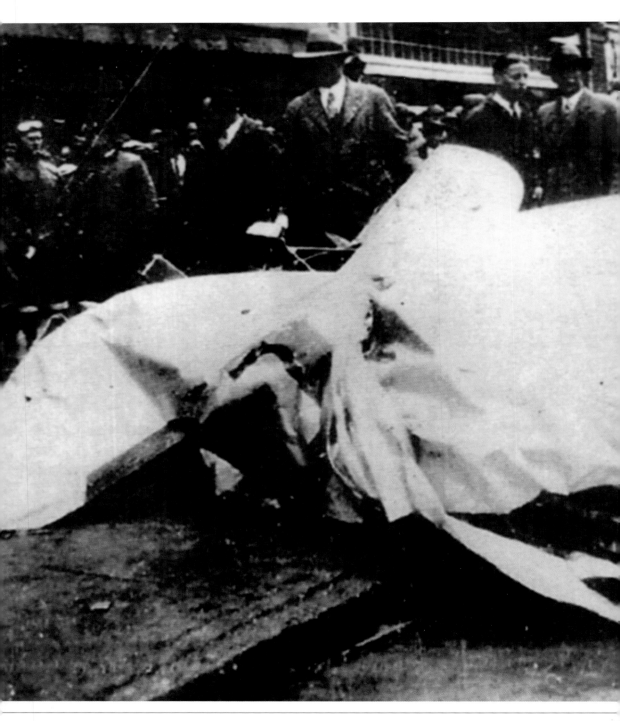

A plane crash on Cherry Street in 1928 ultimately helped Nu-Way prove it had gone by that name before a restaurant by the same name in another sta

(Photo courtesy of The Macon Telegraph)

The Name Game

No one knows if Clyde E. Murphy ever ate a Nu-Way hot dog.

But his name is a sad footnote in the chronicles of the city's oldest restaurant.

On February 18, 1928, one of the most tragic events in Macon's history happened just around the corner from the Nu-Way on Cotton Avenue. It was a Saturday, and downtown was filled with shoppers. A plane from a local air show at Miller Field went into a tailspin and nose-dived into the crowded Cherry Street, injuring more than a dozen people. Both pilots and a pedestrian were killed.

The pedestrian who was killed was a blacksmith named Clyde E. Murphy. He left behind a wife and four children. Members of the community started a "Murphy Fund" for the family.

A story on the front page of the now-defunct *The Macon News* afternoon newspaper on February 24, 1928, reported $141 had been collected.

Gus Baches, who was a co-owner of the Nu-Way at the time, donated $20 to the fund, making him the second-largest individual contributor.

Fast-forward fifty years. By 1978, Nu-Way's front office staff began discussing the importance of pursuing a federal trademark for the Nu-Way brand, especially after what had happened with the restaurant's catchy slogan and the name of its popular hamburger.

Until the 1960s, a large hamburger at the Nu-Way was known as a "Big Boy Burger." Apparently, no one realized Shoney's restaurants had already obtained a trademark on the name "Big Boy" for its hamburgers in 1953.

Attorneys from the Nashville-based company approached Nu-Way about the infringement of the word "Big Boy" on its menu. Nu-Way had no federal trademark. It had only registered the name at the local courthouse, along with the name Nu-Way Weiners.

Rather than become tangled in a legal battle, Nu-Way switched the name to "Mega-Burger" and obtained its own federal copyright.

Later, the shoestring was on the other foot when Nu-Way's attorneys discovered some twenty other restaurants using the name "Mega-Burger." A cease-and-desist order was issued because Nu-Way owned the intellectual property rights.

A similar issue surfaced in the late 1960s involving R. J. Reynolds Tobacco Company. It seems Nu-Way's slogan at the time —"I'd Walk a Mile for a Nu-Way"—was several steps too close to Camel cigarette's "I'd Walk a Mile for a Camel."

Once again, Nu-Way backed off and altered its slogan to "I'd Go A Long Way For A Nu-Way."

"It would have cost a lot of money to fight both of those cases," said Dermatas. "So we waved the white flag."

Nu-Way officials already had registered the restaurant's name with the secretary of state's office. They also determined it would be necessary to trademark the name if they ever decided to franchise the restaurant and expand into other states.

There was only one problem. A trademark attorney in Atlanta informed them there already was a Nu-Way restaurant in Wichita, Kansas.

Wichita's Nu-Way Sandwich Shop had opened its doors on July 4, 1930. It also sold hot dogs and bragged about its "world famous root beer and homemade onion rings" the same way Macon's Nu-Way touted its chili dogs and slaw dogs.

There had been other Nu-Ways in Macon, but none were restaurants. A men's clothing store called Nu-Way Exchange was located on Poplar Street in the 1940s. In the 1950s, there was a Nu-Way Laundry on Broadway and a Nu-Way Cleaners on Houston Avenue, and later on Cherry Street.

The territorial rights of another Nu-Way eating establishment did not appear to be threatening from the standpoint of competition, especially since Wichita was 840 miles away. But Nu-Way's ownership believed it would be important to prove they had been in existence fourteen years longer.

That was going to be difficult, though, especially since many of the company's older records had been destroyed in a basement flood.

George Andros never pushed the panic button. He remembered the front-page newspaper story from 1928. Not only did it list co-owner Baches as a contributor to the fund for Murphy's family, but also established that the Macon restaurant had been around a few years before the one in Wichita.

A compromise was worked out between the Nu-Ways, and they continue to coexist across five states.

A framed copy of *The Macon News* dated February 24, 1928, hangs on a wall at the Nu-Way office on Cotton Avenue.

It saved the day. And the name.

Legend has it that Frank Gordy, founder of The Varsity, once stopped at Nu-Way to ask 'what was the deal with our hot dogs?'
(Photo by Ed Grisamore)

What'll You Have?

When it comes to volume, The Varsity will win the numbers game every time.

It is the largest drive-in restaurant in the world, sprawling across two acres and covering an entire city block in downtown Atlanta.

At any given time, there can be 600 cars in the double-deck parking garage and 800 hundred hungry folks inside, lining up to hear the most famous six words on North Avenue: "What'll you have? What'll you have?"

On Saturday afternoons, when Georgia Tech is playing football three blocks away at Bobby Dodd Stadium, as many as 30,000 people will line up for fried pies and naked dogs. And the end zones at the stadium will smell like onion rings until at least the third quarter.

There is no other restaurant on the planet that serves as many hot dogs, hamburgers, French fries, and Coca-Cola products.

The Varsity has become an Atlanta icon, a place that reaches deep into the personal history of those who have ever sipped a Frosted Orange through a red straw.

Frank Gordy was a native of Thomaston, a mill town about forty-five miles west of Macon. He quit college at Georgia Tech after only one semester, and he left complaining there wasn't any place near campus where you could get something good, fast, and cheap to eat.

He opened the original Varsity in 1928 on a tiny lot and sold sandwiches.

George Andros was part of his own tradition at Macon's Nu-Way for seventy years, starting as a curb boy in the spring of 1929.

He would tell the story about how a man named Frank Gordy stopped by and introduced himself as the owner of a sandwich shop on North Avenue in Atlanta.

"Mr. Gordy was selling pimento cheese and chicken salad at his restaurant, and he wanted to know what was the deal with our hot dogs," said Andros's nephew, Spyros Dermatas.

Whatever trade secrets Gordy was able to cull from the Nu-Way folks, the rest is hot dog history. The Varsity may have lapped its little brother in terms of universal appeal, but Dermatas is convinced it came at the expense of quality for quantity.

"They quit grilling their weiners and started boiling them," he said. "It's a lot easier to boil them and then just pluck them out. When you grill, you have to roll the weiners and put the oil on them and watch them carefully. It's a lot more labor intensive.

"The Varsity just became more interested in sheer volume. When it exploded from a small restaurant to a bigger restaurant and then the world's largest drive-in, then the big issue was the mechanics of putting out that much food, whether it was the way they cut the potatoes or made the hot dogs or chili. It was really an unprecedented phenomenon."

Of course, Dermatas and co-owner Jim Cacavias both went to Georgia Tech in the 1970s, so it was inevitable they would make the short trip across the bridge at I-75 and eat at what students affectionately called "The V."

"It was part of the Tech tradition," said Dermatas. "Someone would come in your room and ask if anyone wanted to make a 'V' run. And the food was good. Maybe not as good as the Nu-Way, but it was good. I was in awe. I have great respect for that family because of what they have accomplished. When I would go in there and see that picture of Mr. Gordy on the wall, it kind of reminded me of what James Mallis did in 1916.

"So I had admiration, just like Alexander the Great. He had the greatest respect for his enemies."

Southern to the Bone

"I was weaned on a steady diet of barbecue sandwiches, Brunswick stew, and sweet tea from Old Clinton Barbecue. During my teen years, I wolfed down chili dogs and slaw-capped dogs from the Nu-Way in Macon."

—John T. Edge, from the book *Southern Belly: The Ultimate Food Lover's Companion to the South*

Old Clinton Bar-B-Q was just down the road from his mailbox, and his five-speed Schwinn practically knew the way by heart.

John T. Edge would ride his bicycle there, park his two wheels at the end of the gravel parking lot, shuffle across the sawdust on the front porch, and wash down a pork sandwich and a Brunswick stew with an Orange Crush.

Although there was a pig on the large sign out front—the one with "Best in Georgia" beneath it—there was no need for him to bring his piggy bank. He ate there so often his family carried a line of credit.

Still, a young man does not live on barbecue alone. Edge regularly carried his taste buds twelve miles south from Gray to Macon. His father, John T. Edge Sr., worked downtown, and Edge was dropped off at his dad's office in the afternoons after school. He was supposed to quietly do his homework. Sometimes, on the way over, he took a hungry detour to the Nu-Way.

He usually got the chili dog. Later on, as his palate and his plate grew more sophisticated, he had them top it off with the creamy slaw.

"It was my way of rationalizing it was healthier," he said, laughing.

His father would also let him tag along on trips to Gandy's Pool Hall on Cherry Street, where Edge was introduced to the gastronomic delights of a scrambled dog.

"Thinking back, those were both iconic Macon foods," he said.

The pool hall is gone, just a memory for those who pulled red dogs from giant puddles of chili topped with the crunch of oyster crackers. By popular demand, and to fill a local void, Nu-Way eventually added the revered scrambled dog to its menu.

Edge still meanders to Cotton Avenue almost every time he comes to Macon because he admittedly still has those insatiable Nu-Way cravings. It's like a request on the jukebox that must be played.

The Cotton Avenue Nu-Way still looks much the way he remembers it. His ten-year-old son, Jess, a chip off the old potato, has developed the same affinity for Nu-Ways.

"He loves the color of the red weinie and the flavor of the chili," said Edge. "He's not at the age where he feels guilty about not eating vegetables."

Edge lives in Oxford, Mississippi, the college town William Faulkner made the literary capital of the South. That is somehow appropriate, since *The Miami Herald* once ordained him as the "Faulkner of Southern food."

He serves as director of the Southern Foodways Alliance, an institute of the Center for the Study of Southern Culture at Ole Miss. He has chewed his way through the South and is the author of ten books, including *Southern Belly*, a fun-filled grub tour of Dixie.

He has been a "culinary curator" for National Public Radio's weekend edition of *All Things Considered.* The *New York Times* and The Food Network routinely solicit his opinion on everything from fried-green tomatoes to buttermilk biscuits. *USA Today* once described him as a "studious chowhound." The man did, after all, write his Master's thesis on potlikker.

Hot dogs normally don't get mentioned in the same breath with Southern staples such as barbecue, grits, turnip greens, and tea cakes. But that doesn't mean they don't cover Dixie like the dewdrops.

"It is the all-American food, but a Nu-Way is distinctly Southern when it is smothered with chili and topped with coleslaw," Edge said. "In the South, slaw is like our salad. Long before we were eating Romaine lettuce, we were having coleslaw with our barbecue and putting chili sauce on our hot dogs."

The lunch crowd at Nu-Way provides the kind of backdrop Edge relishes in his ongoing storytelling of the history and culture of Southern food. The place is breaded in history and deep-fried in tradition. There are no cookie-cut customers spread across the counter.

"A hot dog with chili is a working man's lunch," he said. "And a Nu-Way isn't something God intended for you to eat at home. It is meant to be eaten at the counter or booth, a red weinie cooked on a flat grill with slaw and chili. If you eat it at home, you've missed the point."

John T. Edge, who cut his teeth on Nu-Ways while growing up in Jones County, is one of the nation's most well-respected writers on the culture of food
(Photo by Yvonne Boyd, courtesy of John T. Edge)

Former Georgia Governor Sonny Perdue considers a Nu-Way hot dog an essential part of his diet (Photo courtesy of Nu-Way)

Blessed Be the Fries that Bind

"My family would go to Macon every Saturday to go shopping in the 1950s. We would eat at the Nu-Way on Cherry Street. It was a tradition. I would always get a chili dog. They hadn't started the chili slaw dog. I love the chili dogs. A lot of people have a hard time with the red weiner, but it has a distinctive taste.

"I had Nu-Way cater the luncheon for my staff on my last day in office. It was authentic for me. I couldn't think of anything more appropriate. We have had a lot of great restaurants founded in Georgia—The Varsity, Chick-fil-A, Waffle House—but Nu-Way is my hometown restaurant."

—Sonny Perdue
Bonaire, Georgia
Governor of Georgia (2003–2011)

• • •

"Nu-Way is something Sonny grew up with. To him, there is nothing that can touch a Nu-Way hot dog.

"I went to high school in Atlanta, so I was used to The Varsity. Sonny introduced me to Nu-Way when we were dating. All our children grew up loving Nu-Way. When he would bring them to Atlanta, it was like a little bit of home up here."

—Mary Perdue
Bonaire, Georgia
First Lady of Georgia (2003–2011)

"Nu-Way is hallowed. I would give up an organ to have a miniature version of their neon sign in my basement. The double scrambled dog is a gift from God, and to visit the original location on Cotton Avenue is like visiting the Cooperstown of hot dogs.

"I once delivered a sackful to an acquaintance of mine who was originally from Macon but living in South Carolina. It just so happened he had business in Atlanta and asked if I would be so kind as to bring him five 'all the way.' He ate three the next day for lunch and took the other two and placed under his seat of his car just so he could smell them on the drive back."

—George Fisher
Macon, Georgia

• • •

"My father, Lagrand Hobby, owned the Georgia Baking Company, which was right next door to Nu-Way. We supplied their bread and buns. There was a hole in the wall between the two buildings. The buns would come right out of the oven and cool, and then they would pass them through the hole. Nu-Way had its own machine to slice the buns. As a boy, I can remember watching Mr. [John] Cacavias and Mr. [Nick] Dermatas in the back of the Nu-Way stirring the chili with those big paddles.

"When I was nine years old, we would play basketball at the YMCA on Saturday mornings. Then we would go across the street and run all the way to the top floor of the Banker's Building and back down. We would then see how many Nu-Ways we could eat before we went down to the Ritz Theatre to watch a movie. I could always eat four, all the way, with extra salt. I still say it's the best hot dog in the world. Nu-Way is in a class by itself."

—Steve Hobby
Macon, Georgia

• • •

There is More than One Way to Spell Wiener

"My grandparents lived at the top of Cherry Street. My grandfather loved the railroad and would walk down Cherry Street to the Terminal Station to watch both the trains and the people. I would sometimes go with him, and he would always time it so we could go over to Nu-Way.

"My daddy loved Westerns, and if there was a decent movie on Friday nights, we would go to the 41 Drive-In. We would always have to stop at the Nu-Way on Houston Avenue and get a sack of Nu-Ways.

"I still have a tradition of eating them every Saturday. All the way with extra onions. Both of my children were born on a Saturday, so I guess that's a tradition, too.

"When Katie Beth was born in 1975, Pam was in labor that Saturday. I left with some friends to go to the Nu-Way. I knew it didn't take long to eat a Nu-Way, and I did get back in time, but Pam still was panicking.

"It was different with Matthew in 1981. I had been elected mayor and had a phone in my car. Pam had been having contractions for a week but wasn't having any that day. I thought it would be fine, so I went with a friend to the Nu-Way at Napier Square. As soon as I left the house her contractions got so bad she couldn't even stand up. She called and told me I had better get home. It was close. Matthew was born forty-five minutes after we got to the hospital. She told me she thought she was going to have to birth the baby herself while I ate one more hot dog."

—George Israel
Mayor of Macon (1980–1988)

• • •

"I waitressed most of my young life at both Bloomfield and Napier Square. I started wrapping hot dogs and hamburgers in the back when I was four years old. My mom was the assistant manager, and my aunt and uncle were managers. I remember picking up buckets of onions in the back of my aunt's car when I was sixteen and smelling like onions for days!

"My aunt never called me by my name, just 'kid' and ran a very tight ship. During a rush, when cars would line up all the way out in the street at Napier

Cotton Avenue as it looked in the 1930s. The Nu-Way is on the right (Photo courtesy of The Macon Telegraph)

Square, she would ask us all, 'What's the hold-up?' and promptly send me out into the street to take and deliver orders.

"We had awesome regular customers who came in for coffee and would leave three times the cost of the coffee as a tip because they knew we really worked hard there. We had an old-fashioned cash register that would not add the items and tax. You had to figure it up in your head and punched in the total to open the register. Nu-Way had an awesome system though, where most items were a standard price (like 55 cents for a hot dog, hamburger, fries, Coke) and a chart on the wall with prices plus tax for multiple items. We stayed so busy and figured this so many times in one day, that it only took about a day to memorize the price scale, even when they changed prices. And without a fancy cash register and making change on the street, we had to know how to count correct change, something that seems to be out of fashion in today's world.

"It was not uncommon, though illegal, for my aunt to throw me the keys to her Cadillac when I was fourteen years old and tell me to go downtown and pick up a bucket of onions, pickles, etc. 'The Greeks,' as she referred to Harry [Andros] and the rest, were not aware of this, of course. We were paid in cash in a little yellow envelope each week, with the breakdown of our wages written out on the envelope, minus our meal tickets. (You could eat your wages pretty quickly, and my aunt never missed someone chewing on something and asked immediately if you filled out a meal ticket!) I cannot remember a day that I left there at closing when I did not smell of onions. I also frequently went and dropped the bank bag at the bank. The Nu-Way was run very efficiently. The customer was always right, no matter what."

—Angela Dawn
Gainesboro, Tennessee

• • •

"My dad, George Murphy, was born in 1918 and passed away in 1988. He graduated from Lanier High School and served in the Army in World War II. When he returned from the war as a decorated veteran with Purple Hearts and various medals, the first thing he wanted when he arrived in Macon was a Nu-Way weiner, like he ate in his teenage years.

"After he and my Mom married in the late 1940s, my dad's office was next to the courthouse. He would eat lunch at the Nu-Way on Cotton Avenue practically every day for close to forty years, even after his office moved out of downtown.

"Two things I most remember from my dad's funeral were the minister saying he appreciated my dad signing his paycheck (dad was the church treasurer), and that he never ate lunch at Nu-Way on Cotton Avenue when my Dad wasn't there at the counter."

—Beverly Murphy Bell
Concord, North Carolina

• • •

"When I first ran for mayor of Macon in 2007, I promised to do things a "new way," i.e., do things together for a change. The theme seemed to be catching on, but oh so slowly, until we thought of the idea of giving a coupon for a Nu-Way hot dog. They loved it! When I would go door-to-door campaigning and hand out other election information, I was asked numerous times if I 'had any more of those coupons.' This time (in 2011), people have started asking me whether I still had a 'new way of doing things' and they always seem to perk up when they hear about the candidate with the 'new way.'"

—Robert Reichert
Mayor of Macon

• • •

"Our trips to the Nu-Way are a family tradition. I remember, as a boy, going to the Nu-Way with my grandparents. In more recent years, my family has been spending our Saturday lunch hour eating at the Nu-Way on Cotton Avenue for more than six years.

"My wife, Becky, who grew up on The Varsity dog, has now converted. Our boys, Lee IV and Michael, have grown up looking forward to the familiar, smiling faces behind the counter and the comfort of simply good food.

"Beyond Saturdays, we have toted coolers full of 'all the way, without' to Boy Scout camp, family gatherings, and all the way to the British Virgin Islands aboard a sailboat on family vacations, slowly showing off the world's best hot dog.

"For sure, they will be a part of future graduation parties and wedding receptions. Our older boy has made Nu-Way the theme in many school art projects and even made his Cub Scout Pinewood derby in honor of a Nu-Way hot dog; all of which are displayed in the family game room. Tradition, family, comfort, and original taste…that's Nu-Way."

—Lee Oliver III
Macon, Georgia

◆ ◆ ◆

"In coming from Atlanta to Macon in 1966, I thought that you ordered hot dogs in response to the query: 'What'll ya have?' (a la The Varsity). My parents, however, both Mercer graduates, told me about the Nu-Way, and it was love at first bite.

"While in law school at Mercer, I clerked with the firm of Byrd, Groover & Buford in 1973–1974, and part of the law clerk's duties, in addition to preparing writs of certiorari for the Supreme Court, was making runs to Nu-Way to buy lunch for the lawyers and staff which was served on the library conference table. That is when the addiction really started.

"Through the years, Denmark Groover, Jr. and I kidded about Nu-Ways whenever we met. As he lay in the hospital during his final illness in 2001, I went by to see Spyros, and carried Mr. Groover a Nu-Way hat in recognition of many "weiners" enjoyed together over the years. He was proud of it and kept it on the bedside table.

"In 1998, I experienced a medical problem referred to as atrial fibrillation which, in my case, manifested itself in a rapid and uncontrollably fluctuating heartbeat which landed me in the hospital one Sunday afternoon. The next day, the cardiologist treating me at the Medical Center did a heart catheterization to see if there were any blockages. I received a glowing report about mid-afternoon that I not only did

Judge Lamar Sizemore was treated to a surprise 60th birthday party at the Nu-Way on Northside.
(Photo courtesy of the Sizemore family)

There is More than One Way to Spell Wiener

not have a blockage, but he could not find any evidence of plaque in my arteries, at all. This was a report worthy of celebrating, and it meant my condition could then be controlled by medication alone.

"Shortly after receiving this good news, my friend Don Faulk called as he was coming back into town from a meeting in Atlanta, and said he was on the way to my hospital room where Merry and Sandy were keeping watch. He asked if he could bring me anything, and I'm sure he had in mind a newspaper or a book, but I told him that since there was no sign of plaque in my arteries, I was 'good to go' and wanted to celebrate by eating two "weiners" all the way. Even though the doctor would not let me sit up for six hours following this catheterization, I managed to eat 'two all the way' while laying flat on my back. Not exactly on the hospital recommended dietary plan, but they never tasted better.

"On my sixtieth birthday in November 2008, my son and daughter were in town with their families, including a total of four grandchildren, and as always, they wanted to go to the Nu-Way at Northside and Forest Hill (Nu-Way No. 7) for a meal. Usually we did this for lunch on Saturday, but they lobbied for Saturday evening. I went along with the plan, and was sitting in the front seat of my son's car as we pulled into the parking lot off of Forest Hill, when I saw a crowd of people standing in front of the Nu-Way in the parking lot carrying posters and mounted placards, obviously picketing the Nu-Way. I nearly lost it! I told Rick to get over there quick so we could see who those idiots were, and if necessary, I was going to check with the sheriff's office to see if they had a permit to picket our favorite eatery. As we drew closer, I began to recognize the faces of these protesters, and realized they were all dear friends who obviously had taken leave of their senses. Then I began to read what was on the placards and realized that this was a surprise birthday celebration for me. The placards contained such things as 'Nu-Way reserves booth in honor of Sizemore!' 'Eight more lanes for Forest Hill...Lamar goes to Nu-Way often!' 'Neighbors in uproar, Sizemore to open Nu-Way franchise on Vista Circle!' That was not the only surprise of the evening. When we parked the car and walked up to the front door surrounded by friends, I realized that there were tables placed diagonally across the sidewalk decorated for a birthday and with candles lit on each table. You have never lived until you've had Nu-Way by candle-light on the sidewalk with friends and family! That is one birthday I will never forget. Frankly I lost count of how many hot dogs 'all the way' I had that night.

"If a restaurant, or a meal, can be part of a family's history and tradition, the Nu-Way is part of ours, and friends come no dearer than Spyros and Emily, who understand that they and their business are a special part of our family."

—Lamar Sizemore
Retired Judge
Macon, Georgia

• • •

"Memories of my mama's relish for Nu-Ways go back to 1947, when I was about five years old. My high-society aunt, after a downtown shopping trip, led us to a narrow, white-floored hot dog place on Cotton Avenue, where she introduced my displaced-Yankee mother to Macon's superior answer to the Coney Island weiner. We hat-wearing, gloved ladies didn't eat at the chrome counter on twirly stools, but ordered from a booth, where I played with a wall-mounted jukebox selector.

"Fast-forward through a million hot dogs and ask my ninety-seven-year-old mother where to go for lunch, and she will still say 'the Nu-Way!' As downtown sidewalk steps got too hard for her, Mom and I ate take-outs in my car and, when that got too messy, a walker helped her get to a booth at Zebulon Road's newer store. These days—about twice a month—she rolls happily into the food court, in her nursing home wheelchair, for her usual. We've come a long way with Nu-Way."

—Julie Bragg
Macon, Georgia

A Nu-Way business card from the 1930s (Photo courtesy of Nu-Way)

"I drove for more than twenty-four hours, from New Mexico, to have my birthday luncheon at the Bloomfield Nu-Way. Keith Layson, who shares the same birth date with me, has celebrated his birthday at that Nu-Way for more than thirty years. We had a blast! Keith, Lisa Rountree Flury, Janna McWhorter, and I all decided we wanted to get our former Burghard Elementary School classmates together for a reunion, of sorts. We had all lost touch through the years but had reconnected on Facebook. So, we thought, for the purpose of nostalgia, we would make our meeting site one from our past. And what better place than the Nu-Way on the corner of Rocky Creek and Bloomfield? It was the only business that was still in business in the same location as when we were kids.

"We agreed on a date, then made the hours long enough to accommodate everybody's schedule. We posted the invitation to all our classmates on Facebook. We had many classmates and a few neighborhood friends who attended another nearby school to come by. And we had fun! I can't help but smile, thinking about those poor, unsuspecting patrons and Nu-Way staff, when the whole group of us showed up and filled every seat in the place! It was 'standing room only' for about an hour!

"Keith and I talked about how he and I share the same birthday, and how he's always spent his birthday at Nu-Way. He even has his own stool there. It's his tradition that, for his birthday, he goes to Nu-Way, to his favorite stool, and orders his favorite Nu-Way combo."

—Sue Burch
Truth or Consequences, New Mexico

• • •

"I was born and raised in the Byron area and moved to Alaska in 2002. Every time we would come back, which wasn't often enough, we'd buy about twenty hot dogs and put them in a cooler to take back with us. We came back a few years ago for our daughter's wedding and stayed in the area less than twenty-four hours, but we did get our hot dog fix! We left the wedding reception, changed clothes, loaded the rental car, and went directly to Nu-Way and then the airport.

"These are really the only hot dogs I love to eat. My grandfather, Albert 'Pop' Pratt, would take me to Nu-Way at Stantom Plaza in Warner Robins, and we would sit at the counter. I loved those spin-around seats. My Pop would have his hands full keeping me on it as I would make myself very dizzy doing that until the chili dogs arrived. I was fascinated with all the chrome in the place! It was such a great experience to be in a real 'diner' type of establishment. I would open one up tomorrow given the chance."

—Kathy Pratt Kodra
Murphy, North Carolina

• • •

"The four years I lived in Tallahassee, the thing I missed the most about Macon was Nu-Way. The only thing they had similar was something called Wiener King. They may have spelled the name correctly, but their hot dogs were nothing like Nu-Way. So, once when my mom came for a visit, she brought me a sack of ten Nu-Way hot dogs, double-wrapped, so that I could freeze them and eat them later. But I learned that a nuked Nu-Way a week-or-so later is not the same as when they are fresh. And I'm convinced that the smell of micro-waved Nu-Way hot dogs is the reason it took me more than three years to sell my house after I moved back to Macon."

—Ben Sandifer
Macon, Georgia

• • •

"My mother, Virginia McClure, grew up on Boulevard. When we used to visit my grandmother, we would always go down to Nu-Way. We lived on Oxford, and I would sometimes get in trouble because I would ride my bike all the way over to the Nu-Way on Northside Drive in the summertime.

"I got married on March 28, 1998. It was a late-afternoon wedding. My best friend, Hyatt Hall, and I went over and got Nu-Ways for lunch. We ate them right behind the Chi-Ches-Ter's. We laughed and said it was my last meal as a bachelor. He took me back to the hotel where I could shower and change. So, no, I didn't get a chili stain on my tie.

"The wedding was at the Hay House. I was a few minutes late for the photographs. I was so full I didn't even eat supper that night.

"Every March 28, we have a tradition of having lunch at the Nu-Way. My wife, Tonya, and I take the boys, Chase and Lawson."

—Jeff McClure
Macon, Georgia

• • •

"We have some property at the river. Three years ago, we found a little dog under the deck. We think she may have wandered up from Highway 83. She was precious. We tried to get her to come to us. My husband, Randy, started calling her 'Nu-Way' because she looked like the dog with the little boy on the T-shirt.

"We took her home but I told my daughters (Courtney and Sarah) we were not keeping her. She was nothing but skin and bones. She had ticks and fleas, so we took her to the vet. She's a mutt. She has a little of everything in her. I think she looks a lot like the dog on *Little Rascals*.

"After a week, we fell in love with her so, of course, we kept her. And now she's not just our dog. She's the neighborhood dog. She's a little crazy. She jumps fences and chases cars and birds.

"Everybody knows 'Nu-Way.' I was walking her around the (Rivoli Oaks) neighborhood and a woman came up and said, 'Nu-Way! How have you been?'

"So the dog we were never going to let in the house now lives with us. She thinks she's a person."

—Darlene Brittain
Macon, Georgia

Sarah Brittain plays with the family dog, who answers to the name "Nu-Way"
(Photo courtesy of the Brittain family)

"We used to go to the Nu-Way on Houston Avenue and Cotton Avenue when I was growing up. I left Macon in 1969, went into the Army and went to Vietnam.

"When I was stationed at Fort Bragg, whenever we would go through Macon, I would have make a trip to Nu-Way, and also when I was with the South Carolina National Guard in Columbia.

"Some of my friends from Macon would bring me Nu-Way hot dogs. Once I was at a conference in Atlanta and a friend brought up twenty-five. I was staying with my brother, who lived in Roswell. We feasted on all those Nu-Ways.

"People have asked me why I just leave them in the car. They won't spoil. I like the aroma they leave behind.

"I had an aunt in St. Augustine who died in January. The funeral was in Atlanta. I drove over from South Carolina. The first thing my cousin did when I got to the cemetery was pull out a bag of Nu-Ways. I ate one right there."

—Mike Schulman
Lexington, South Carolina

• • •

"When my husband, Mike Cook, was in Vietnam his mother had Nu-Way hot dogs shipped to him. He was over there in 1969–1970, Army Artillery, and he's not sure now exactly where he was stationed at the time. The chili and hot dogs were canned separately, and there were buns as well. The guys weren't sure the weiners had made the trip OK, so they substituted regular hot dogs, but he says the chili made them taste just fine! The sign said they would ship 'anywhere' and I guess they did!"

—Dorothy B. Cook
Macon, Georgia

"I was a 1953 graduate of Lanier High School and played in the band. After every football parade downtown we went to the Nu-Way. The place was jam packed on parade days, but if you waited you could get your delicious Nu-Way weiner. Lanier High School football parades were nothing compared with the parade in 1952 honoring the newly crowned Miss America from Macon, Georgia, Miss Neva Jane Langley, now Mrs. Bill Fickling. I am sure the crowd at Nu-Way took days to clear out. People were standing outside waiting.

"After moving from Macon I return from time to time and have to get a Nu-Way fix. I introduced my daughter and two grandchildren to Nu-Way so they would not grow up being deprived of that Nu-Way Weiner sensation. When visiting Macon now I get about two dozen 'all the way to go,' freeze them, and take them home to Florida. I wish I had about a half-dozen to eat right now."

—John Henry Pittman
Crestview, Florida

A Nu-Way illustration from the 1960s (Photo courtesy of Nu-Way)

Nu-Way by the Numbers

1. The *New York Times* rated the Nu-Way slaw dog as No.1 in America in July 2002.

2. The first two words ever spoken by beloved cartoon character Mickey Mouse were "Hot dogs!" Mickey discovered his voice as a hot dog vendor in the 1929 short film, *The Karnival Kid.*

3. The number of hot dogs Oprah Winfrey ordered on her visit to Nu-Way in October 2007. (She only ate two and a half.)

4. The number of Nu-Way owners who went by the name of "Gus." There was Gus Psilopoulos (1918–1932), Gus Cacavias (1926–1927), Gus Baches (1928–1929), and Gus Lolos (1932–1958).

5. A nickel was the original cost of a hot dog when Nu-Way opened in 1916. It remained 5 cents until the 1940s.

6. According to the National Hot Dog and Sausage Council, the average hot dog is consumed in six bites.

7. Nu-Way was voted "Best Hot Dog" in a 2007 "Best of the Best" survey by readers of *The Macon Telegraph.*

8. The number of horizontal stripes on the little boy's jacket in the famous Nu-Way logo, painted by former Macon fire chief B. H. Brown.

9. Anthony Weiner is a former U. S. Representative from New York's ninth congressional district. He resigned in June 2011 after a highly publicized sex scandal. He is not affiliated with Nu-Way Weiner Stand, except for the misspelling of his name, of course. (No jokes, please.)

10. Homer's epic Greek poem *The Odyssey* begins after the ten-year Trojan War. It makes the earliest known reference to sausage, the world's first processed food and the great granddaddy of hot dogs.

11. The newest Nu-Way, No. 11, opened at 1215 Russell Parkway in Warner Robins on December 1, 2000.

12. The number of boxes of lollipops in a case for the Nu-Way kids' meals.

13. The number of words in the jingle, "I'd Go a Long Way for a Nu-Way. Woh. Woh. Woh. Yeah. Nu-Way!" It was sung by a quartet known as the Nu-Way Doo-Wops and performed on NBC's *Today* show in 2003.

The Nu-Way Doo-Wops quartet (Photo courtesy of Nu-Way)

14. Owner George Andros was fourteen years old when he started working at Nu-Way as a curb boy in 1929.

15. John Cacavias was the fifteenth owner of Nu-Way.

16. There are sixteen hot dog buns in each pack.

17. There have been seventeen Nu-Way locations opened since the first in 1916.

18. There have been eighteen Nu-Way owners since 1916.

19. It takes nineteen pounds of spices and onions to make one thirty-six-gallon batch of Nu-Way chili sauce.

20. Owner Gus Baches made a $20 donation to the "Murphy Fund" to help the family of a pedestrian killed in a plane crash on Cherry Street in February 1928. The donation was listed in the local newspaper and was a pivotal piece of documentation to help Nu-Way establish proof it had the name before another Nu-Way restaurant in Kansas.

21. George Andros was twenty-one years old when he became a co-owner in 1936.

22. There were twenty-two hot dog restaurants featured on *A Hot Dog Program* on PBS in 1999. Nu-Way's two-minute spot on the show brought it national attention.

23. Each of the nine Nu-Ways goes through an average of twenty-three pounds (2.58 gallons) of chili sauce per day.

24. There are twenty-four slices of white bread in a loaf of Capt. John's Derst Bread, used by Nu-Way for its egg sandwiches; grilled cheese sandwiches; and bacon, lettuce, and tomato sandwiches.

25. There was a twenty-five-year gap between opening the two newest Macon Nu-Ways—Northside Drive (1975) and Zebulon Road (2000).

26. Nu-Way is open for business an average of twenty-six days each month. (It is closed on Sundays and major holidays.)

27. The train made twenty-seven stops when Nu-Way founder James Mallis made the trip from New York City to Macon in 1916.

28. The Nu-Way catering operation averages twenty-eight special orders every month.

29. On the average, each Nu-Way goes through twenty-nine cases of weiners a week. There are 100 weiners in each case.

30. There are thirty pounds of French fries in every case at Nu-Way.

31. How many Mexican-style beans are there in a ten-ounce bowl of chili? If you said thirty-one, then you are a weiner...er, winner.

32. A quart of the renowned chili with beans (thirty-two ounces) will cost you five dollars, three quarters, one dime, two nickels and four pennies. That adds up to $5.99.

33. It is a distance of thirty-three miles from Nu-Way's northernmost store on Zebulon Road to its southernmost restaurant in Fort Valley.

34. Nu-Way sells an average of thirty-four caps, T-shirts, and other merchandise each month.

35. When James Mallis opened the first Nu-Way in 1916, he could walk down Cotton Avenue to the Macon Tea & Coffee Co., and buy a pound of java-mocha blend for 35 cents.

36. According to some of her co-workers, Napier Square manager Makeia Brown has changed her hairstyle and color at least three dozen times since she began working at Nu-Way.

37. The legendary neon sign went up on Cotton Avenue in 1937, famously misspelling the word "W-E-I-N-E-R." The rest is history.

38. The Macon Whoopee hockey team lost thirty-eight games during the 1973–1974 season and folded before the end of the year despite being voted the best all-time team nickname by *Sports Illustrated*. That has absolutely nothing to do with Nu-Way, except that the team was named after a popular song, "Makin' Whoopee," first made famous by singer Eddie Cantor. And Cantor was

a singing waiter in New York in 1916 when he and Jimmy Durante encouraged a man named Nathan Handwerker to open his own Nathan's Famous hot-dog stand in 1916 in the Brooklyn neighborhood of Coney Island. Nathan's is the oldest hot dog stand in America. Macon's Nu-Way is the second-oldest.

39. There are 39 seats in the dining area at the Cotton Avenue restaurant (eleven stools and twenty-eight booth seats.) (Photo courtesy of Nu-Way)

40. Bet you didn't know forty Mega-Burger patties (four ounces each) come in each case. (Maybe it will be a question when you're a contestant on Jeopardy!)

41. During his baseball career, Hank Aaron hit forty-one more home runs (755) than Babe Ruth (714). Perhaps that's because legend has it Ruth once downed twelve hot dogs and eight sodas between games of a double-header.

42. For its first forty-two years (1916–1958), Nu-Way was run as a partnership. The partners were Greek immigrants who would come to America, work a few years, save their money, go back to the old country, and later return to the U.S. and buy an interest in the partnership.

43. When she completed her tour in 1943, actress Marlene Dietrich sold more war bonds than any other celebrity. It was also Dietrich who also once said hot dogs and champagne were her favorite meal.

44. A large drink at Nu-Way is forty-four ounces.

Nothing beats a 44-ounce drink with flaky ice (Photo courtesy of Nu-Way)

45. Each Nu-Way goes through forty-five jelly packs during each breakfast cycle. (If they run out, they're in a real jam.)

46. There were forty-six years separating the founding of Nu-Way and the grand opening of its first suburban store on Houston Avenue in 1962.

47. If inquiring minds want to know how many ounces of mustard bran do each of the Nu-Way restaurants use each day, the answer is forty-seven.

48. Nu-Way opened its second location at 422 Cherry Street in 1948. It closed twenty years later after being damaged by fire that started in an adjoining business, Central Jewelers.

49. Employee Ray Mills had forty-nine different addresses during his thirty-year career with Nu-Way. He gathered no moss.

50. There are fifty pounds in a case of cabbage used to make Nu-Way's blue-ribbon coleslaw.

51. Nu-Way owners wore out fifty-one erasers trying to keep up with all the times Ray Mills moved.

52. Say cheese! Each Nu-Way location uses fifty-two slices of cheese per store during the lunch hour.

53. Fifty-three years after its grand opening in 1916, Nu-Way opened its first franchised location in Warner Robins in February 1969.

54. The average (fifty-four) number of drink holders used at all Nu-Way locations in one day.

55. Nu-Way uses fifty-five-gallon liners in its trash cans.

56. The family "Weiner Wagon" was a '56 Chevrolet Bel Air station wagon.

57. Engineer Carl Hofstadter can be spotted sipping unsweetened tea at the Nu-Way at Napier Square at least fifty-seven times a year.

58. On the fifty-eighth day of the year (February 27) in 2016, Nu-Way will celebrate its one-hundredth anniversary.

59. Whose turn is it to take out the trash? Each Nu-Way location uses an average of fifty-nine trash-can liners every day.

60. There are sixty calories in four tablespoons of ketchup. Do you want fries with that?

61. The number of double-takes Cotton Avenue manager Veronica Smith and her son, Quinn Hollis, did when they were interviewed by Durwood "Mr. Doubletalk" Fincher on a YouTube video in 2010.

62. In 1962, Houston Avenue opened the city's first drive-thru restaurant and one of the first in the state.

63. George Andros was a co-owner for sixty-three of the seventy years he worked at Nu-Way, starting as a part-time waiter in 1929.

64. Crunch time. There are sixty-four bags of potato chips in each case.

65. Nu-Way was incorporated on December 17, 1965.

66. Macon fire chief B. H. Brown retired in October 1966 after joining the department in January 1948. He was a well-known local artist who painted the famous *Boy and Dog* still used today as the Nu-Way logo.

67. Becky Mercuri wrote about Nu-Way on page 67 of *The Great American Hot Dog Book*.

68. The world record for eating hot dogs was set by Joey "Jaws" Chestnut, a professional eater from San Jose, California, who devoured sixty-eight franks in ten minutes at the annual Nathan's Hot Dog Eating Contest on Coney Island in 2009.

69. The last time a Nu-Way opened its doors for business on a Sunday was in 1969.

70. The famous neon sign on Cotton Avenue was in operation for seventy years until it received a facelift in 2007. (Photo courtesy of Nu-Way)

71. In a famous scene from the 1971 movie *Dirty Harry*, Clint Eastwood, still munching on his hot dog, walks out of a diner to apprehend a bank robber. A few years later, as inspector Harry Callahan in the sequel *Sudden Impact*, he tells his partner, "God, this stuff isn't getting to me—the shootings, the knifings, the beatings. Old ladies being bashed in the head for their social security checks. Nah, that doesn't bother me. But you know what does bother me? You know what makes me really sick to my stomach? It's watching you stuff your face with those hot dogs! Nobody, I mean nobody, puts ketchup on a hot dog!"

72. The number of hours Nu-Way hot dogs are frozen before being shipped.

73. Lagrand Hobby, who died in 1973, was owner of the Georgia Baking Company, a longtime supplier of the bread and buns for Nu-Way. For many years, the bakery was located next door to the Nu-Way, and the fresh bread was passed through an opening in the wall.

74. Nu-Way signed the lease to open its first north Macon restaurant at the corner of Forest Hill and Northside Drive in 1974, the same year owner Nick Dermatas died of a heart attack.

75. There is 75 percent lean beef in a Mega-Burger patty.

76. The Cotton Avenue restaurant is open for seventy-six hours each week, from 6 A.M. to 7 P.M. Monday through Friday and 7 A.M. to 6 P.M. on Saturday.

77. Nu-Way was one of the seventy-seven "quirky characters, roadside oddities, and other offbeat stuff" from middle and south Georgia featured in William Schemmel's book *Georgia Curiosities*.

78. As of March 2011, there were seventy-eight different items on the customer menu.

79. It is a distance of seventy-nine miles from store No. 1 on Cotton Avenue to all stores, ending at No. 11 on Russell Parkway in Warner Robins.

80. There are eighty hamburger patties in each ten-pound case.

81. Bonaire native Sonny Perdue, who became the eighty-first governor of Georgia in 2003 (and the first Republican governor since Reconstruction), had Nu-Way cater the luncheon for his staff on his final day in office in January 2011.

82. The estimated number (eighty-two) of Mega-Burgers with cheese and bacon consumed by Mega-Attorney Steve Wilson every year. (Note: Wilson disputes this claim but has no circumstantial evidence.) (Photo courtesy of Nu-Way)

83. Owner John N. Dermatas lived in Room 83 of the Parkland Hotel in 1924.

84. Time for change? The nine Nu-Way locations combine to use eighty-four rolls of coins every day.

85. It is eighty-five miles up I-75 from the entrance to Nu-Way No. 5 off North Avenue in Macon to the parking lot at The Varsity on North Avenue in Atlanta.

86. In 1986, legendary newspaper columnist Lewis Grizzard listed the "Nu-Way Weinie joint in Macon" as one of the world's outstanding restaurants.

87. According to national studies, 87 percent of all hot dog eaters prefer mustard to ketchup.

88. Robert Stribling has been known to devour eighty-eight scrambled dog platters in a fifty-two-week span at Nu-Way No. 7 on Northside Drive.

89. The average number of sips of "Famous Flaky Ice" per thirty-two-ounce drink. (Less if you're really, really thirsty.)

90. The number of breakfast platters (two eggs and sausage) eaten by Virgil Burton at the Napier Square Nu-Way during months that end in either "r" or "y."

91. Uncle Harry Andros was known to perform at least ninety-one "taste tests" a month during his Nu-Way career.

92. In the 1930s, the first two numbers of Nu-Way's four-digit number was "92," as in "9255."

93. An average of ninety-three Mega-Burgers are sold every week at each Nu-Way location.

94. The average number times Nick Dermatas made the chili sauce and barbecue sauce every three months in the early 1970s.

95. The number of weekly discussions by the "crows" early morning crew at the Baconsfield Nu-Way, trying to solve the hitting woes of the Atlanta Braves and all the other problems of the world.

96. Mayor Robert Reichert's 2007 campaign passed out Nu-Way coupons as part of his promise to show the city a "New Way For Macon." Reichert crushed his opponent in the general election with 96 percent of the vote.

97. The average number of bacon, lettuce, and tomato and ham, lettuce, and tomato sandwiches sold each week at all nine Nu-Way locations.

98. The year, 1998, third-generation owner Jim Cacavias returned to Macon and took the reins from his father, John Cacavias.

99. The popular ten-ounce bowl of grits is 99 cents on the breakfast menu.

100. A Nu-Way hot dog is 100 percent beef and pork.

Index